NO BULLSH*T
MONEY ADVICE

Straight-talking strategies
to take control of your cash

Andy Hart

No Bullsh*t Money Advice

ISBN 978-1-915483-76-8

eISBN 978-1-915483-77-5

Audio ISBN 978-1-915483-78-2

Published in 2026 by Right Book Press

Printed in the UK in March 2026

Manufactured by
Sue Richardson Associates Ltd.
Studio 6,
9, Marsh Street
Bristol
BS1 4AA

info@therightbookcompany.com

© Andy Hart

The right of Andy Hart to be identified as the author of this work has been asserted in accordance with the Copyright, Designs and Patents Act 1988.

A CIP record of this book is available from the British Library.

All rights reserved. No part of this book may be reproduced, stored in a retrieval system, or transmitted in any form or by any means, electronic, mechanical, photocopying, recording or otherwise, without the prior written permission of the copyright holder.

Communicating complex financial principles in simple language is a superpower, one that Andy Hart is the best in the UK at wielding. This book will do more than just help you understand money; it will help you connect your finances and your life so that magic happens, and your future will be infinitely more secure and exciting for reading it.

– **Pete Matthew**, CEO, Jacksons Wealth Management and founder of the Meaningful Money project

Andy Hart is a rare voice of clarity in a noisy industry. If you want straight answers and practical wisdom about money, you'll find it here.

– **Jason Butler**, serial investor and business adviser

Finally, a money book that isn't just about money, but about the people who it belongs to.

– **Rory Sutherland**, author of *Alchemy* and vice chair, Ogilvy

Andy Hart has a rare talent for cutting through the noise and delivering practical, straight-talking financial advice. His content is always packed with value, and this book promises to be no different – clear, actionable and no-nonsense.

– **Warren Shute**, CFP and author of *The Money Plan*

The world of personal finance can feel like navigating a minefield with advice being thrown at you from all directions. This book gets to the point and offers a step-by-step guide to help you understand personal finance and use your resources better for the life you really want.

– **Tina Weeks**, founder, Serenity Financial Planning

If you are looking for straight-up money advice without the jargon, this is the book for you. Andy Hart has been at the forefront of promoting best financial practice for families for over a decade. His guidance will help you accumulate wealth and live the life you have always dreamed about.

– **Carl Widger**, managing director, Metis Ireland

This book is provided for information purposes only and doesn't constitute financial, investment, tax, legal or any other form of regulated advice. Although I am a regulated financial adviser, I don't know your personal circumstances, financial position, objectives or attitude to risk and nothing in this book should be taken as personal advice. Any examples or opinions are illustrative only and should not be relied upon when making financial decisions. Before acting on any information contained here, you should consider its suitability for your own situation and seek independent advice from a suitably qualified financial adviser or other appropriate professional. All investing carries risk and any actions you take as a result of reading this book are your own responsibility.

Contents

Foreword — vii
Preface — 1

1. Let's get started — 7
2. Key principles — 19
3. Taking control — 29
4. Investing — 67
5. Partnering and finding support — 129

Bonus section — 145
References — 149
About the author — 151

Foreword

I've had the pleasure of knowing Andy Hart for more than 15 years. In that time, I've seen him evolve from a smart, inquisitive financial adviser into one of the most influential voices in the world of personal finance and behavioural money management. Andy's journey has been anything but conventional – and that's precisely what makes him, and this book, so compelling.

One of Andy's greatest strengths is his ability to take complex financial concepts – things that often baffle or intimidate people – and explain them in a way that is clear, practical and, crucially, bullshit free.

He doesn't hide behind industry jargon or use convoluted charts to sound clever. He simply tells the truth, in plain English, with a healthy dose of humour and humility. That, in itself, is a rare thing.

No Bullsh*t Money Advice is the distillation of everything Andy stands for: clarity, truth and an unwavering commitment to helping people actually *understand* money. Not just how it works in theory – but how to master it in real life.

In these pages, you'll find insights that challenge the status quo, debunk financial myths and guide you towards real financial success – not the Instagram version, not the spreadsheet version, but the version that gives you peace of mind, confidence and long-term freedom.

Andy is one of those rare individuals who not only serves clients at the highest level, but also devotes himself to raising the standard of the entire financial planning profession. Through his work with Maven Money and Humans Under Management, he's had an extraordinary impact.

Humans Under Management isn't just a conference – it's a movement. Andy's been at the forefront of educating advisers globally on behavioural finance, encouraging them to see their clients not just as portfolios but as human beings with emotions, fears, habits and dreams.

The financial advice world is, frankly, better because Andy's in it. And speaking from personal experience, I can say that with absolute conviction – because Andy is also *my* financial planner.

I trust him to guide me, challenge me and tell me the truth, even when it's uncomfortable. He's not only a sounding board for my own decisions, but also someone I often refer to when I need perspective on how to approach the most important financial conversations.

This book is more than just a guide – it's a manifesto. It's for people who want real answers, who are tired of the noise and who want to take control of their money without losing their minds in the process. Whether you're a complete beginner or someone who's been around the financial block a few times, Andy has something valuable to say to you.

So, as you turn the pages ahead, prepare to laugh, nod and occasionally squirm. You might even have a few uncomfortable light bulb moments. But that's the beauty of Andy's style – he cuts through the noise and gets straight to the heart of what really matters.

Enjoy the ride. You're in safe hands.

Alan Smith, CEO, Capital Partners, London

Preface

Before I introduce myself properly, let's get one thing out of the way. Yes, I'm a financial adviser, and so, despite some of the things I say about the industry (which is a young profession) in this book, I will always advocate for a conversation with one of my colleagues.

My name is Andy Hart. I'm in my early forties, a proud father of twins, Poppy and Mylo, and I've spent my entire career working in money – not chasing it, but understanding it, helping people make better decisions with it and, most importantly, protecting them from the forces that so often conspire to separate them from it.

My North Star has always been simple: better financial outcomes for real people. Not the industry. Not the institutions. Not the noise. Just people. And here's the uncomfortable truth: my industry – the world of financial services – is paid handsomely for you not knowing what to do. Complexity is profitable. Confusion keeps the machine running. But it rarely serves you, and it certainly won't serve the next generation. That's why I've written this book. I want Poppy and Mylo to grow up in a world where managing money is built on pristine simplicity – where strong financial foundations and confident decisions are the norm, not the exception.

But I also know we're fighting against human nature: emotion, bias, fear, greed, procrastination – they all get in the way. And the financial world is more than happy to exploit that. This book is my attempt to fight back and give you clarity, not jargon; empowerment, not dependency; and help you see that managing your money well isn't just possible – it's far simpler than you've been led to believe.

I've written this book as your guide to take you from money uncertainty to money confidence. I've spent 20 years of my life working with everyday people and educating them about their money and what to do with it.

I should also note that I'm British and have spent my entire career as a financial adviser here in the UK, so my advice *is* specific to this country, in terms of pensions, tax requirements and so on. However, if you're based elsewhere in the world, the broad advice still stands. And, of course, there will be equivalent tax schemes and savings options in your own country. But please do your own research on these.

This book is intended for absolute beginners who want to get a handle on their money, but will also guide experienced investors and dispel myths they have around creating wealth. Whether you are a beginner or have more experience, you want financial independence – which means you've accumulated enough resources to support your lifestyle in later life without having to ever work again.

Whatever stage you're at, by picking up this book you're ready to take control of your finances and make sure you and your family are secure and comfortable. Maybe you've dabbled with investing and not seen the returns you were hoping for. Perhaps you've had a couple of kids and see the importance of a stable future for them, or maybe you're heading towards retirement and need to organise your finances. Or perhaps you're just ready to take control of your money. Whichever stage of life you're in, I can help.

Let me be your guide away from being financially unschooled and towards better financial management.

Habits, mindset and conflicting advice

The reason most people falter financially is due to their habits and their mindset. These can be worked on. Working through my guidance in this book will lead to behavioural change that will help you employ good habits around your money and ultimately to investing in your future.

As I've mentioned, the money industry is designed to confuse you and profit from you. I'm here to stop this happening and I hope I've created the only book you'll need to read or listen to about money. It will put you on a direct path to money wisdom and investing success, and you'll be motivated to continue to work on your financial plan over your lifetime.

Some of the things I write may surprise you. I'm not being provocative for the sake of it, but that's the effect they might have. A part of this direct approach is to give you truthful, honest advice. This will include uncomfortable truths, not comfortable lies.

I'm not going to just tell you what you want to hear – there are more than enough people doing that already. This book is partly a response to them, a response to a culture of needing to be nice and pandering to sensitivities instead of actually helping people.

I'm extremely proud that someone gave my podcast this review:

> **Repeatative** 3y ago
> ★☆☆☆☆
> Not much new in each episode, basically buy global trackers

If people paid more attention to the advice I give over and over again, they'd be much better off!

We're all grown-ups and sometimes we need to be reminded that we have to behave like one, which means taking responsibility, acting on the right advice, even if it pushes us out of our comfort zone, and not running a mile if someone says something we disagree with.

We all tell the odd white lie every now and again, but financial advisers telling lies about finance to keep people happy is a disastrous and reckless approach that's storing up big problems for the future. It fans the flames of bad financial behaviour and encourages us to make the wrong decisions at crucial moments and to repeat them over and over again.

I want to stop this happening and to encourage you to make the right choices based on a clear understanding of your situation and what's at stake. Keeping you happy, rather than well informed, isn't the only reason why some financial advisers are scared to speak the truth – perpetuating myths about finance and investing also keeps them in a job.

Believe it or not, for a variety of reasons, some people involved in financial advice, financial services or financial media have no interest in your long-term financial wellbeing. It suits them to keep you mystified, underinformed, confused or frightened because it means they can keep on doing what they do. Whether that's selling to you or scaring you, they all have their self-interested reasons. Their careers rely on it (see, I wasn't joking when I said I was direct).

I might at times sound angry or exasperated, but that's because this situation often makes me angry or exasperated. Don't be scared or put off by that. Get angry with me, and let's do something about it together. I dream of a world filled with financially savvy, switched-on individuals.

Ultimately, I'm on your side – you'll see that as you work through the book. By tackling each topic slowly and delving deeper as you go, just like getting physically fit, you will start with small steps and build.

There'll be no long technical theories, just useful insights and lessons explained clearly in terms you can understand. I'll be honest but not rude; smart but not patronising – and give you the knowledge to approach your own financial decisions in the same manner.

Let's get going.

1
Let's get started

Attitudes to money are often shaped by the internal story we tell ourselves. It's an ongoing dialogue in our minds, where we frame money in either a positive or negative light based on our experiences, beliefs and emotions.

These stories can stem from past experiences, cultural influences or even our upbringing, and they play a significant role in how we perceive and manage our finances. Sometimes the philosophy we adopt is a useful one that will make us successful, happy and productive.

But at other times it's not, and we either concede defeat – 'I'm bad with money', 'I'm unlucky with money', 'I don't do money' – or have an over-inflated belief in our own abilities to make the right financial decisions.

It's important to recognise that these internal narratives exist. The good news is that they are not fixed in you! They can be rewritten. By recognising and challenging your poor behavioural patterns, you can create new, empowering money stories that support better financial decisions.

Ultimately, the only person who can change and improve your relationship with money is you. The first thing you need to do is recognise where you are in life and what you know. And by the time you've finished this book, you'll feel confident with your wealth-building and be ready to get to financial independence (we'll look at this in more detail throughout the book).

Myths

Whether we're good with it or bad with it isn't the only type of money story we tell ourselves. We might convince ourselves that we can only be happy if we buy that new car right away. Or we need to reduce our pension contributions so we can treat ourselves more often today rather than defer this pleasure until the future, because, who knows, we might get hit by a bus tomorrow.

These are stories too. Stories we write and tell ourselves to justify a decision we've often already made.

We tend to think of people who are financially successful as being somehow different from the rest of us, as if they have been gifted something that wasn't available to everyone. We talk of people being 'good with money' as if one day a finite amount of these skills was shared out between us all and only a lucky few won the metaphorical lottery. Then the rest of us just shrug, accept our lot and get on with our normal, OK-but-not-fantastic-with-money lives.

Many reasons are given as the cause of people losing, failing to accumulate or not having enough money: inflation; poor investment returns; house price deflation and negative equity; the high cost of debt; low wages; debt crises; and political regimes (think austerity). I'm going to level with you here: not a single one of these things should concern you.

Why should they? You have absolutely no control or influence over these factors – despite being constantly warned against such things as if they can be changed. Over and above all these, and any other outside influences you might think affect your ability to build and grow your personal wealth, the most significant factor in this equation is *you*.

For you are a human, hard wired to make terrible financial decisions and destroy your own wealth-building potential. To believe otherwise is simply arrogance. We are all born with zero financial knowledge. I was. You were. The world's most successful investors and businesspeople, such as Warren Buffett, Jeff Bezos and Oprah Winfrey, all were. But the difference between them and the majority of us is that they didn't stay that way. They did something about it. They educated themselves and became successful with money. They broke 'the cycle'.

What do I mean by this? Breaking the cycle is key – scary money stories and bad habits are passed down through generations. This is what I want to change for you: instead of poor money habits passing down, I want successful habits to pass down.

You can be successful with money if you want it enough and if you're willing to do the work to build your money brain.

Let me share an example. I was in a taxi and chatting with the driver, as you do. When he found out I was a financial adviser, he launched into a speech about how he lived by his grandad's financial advice:

'My grandad always used to say, "If you've got any spare cash, put it in a shoebox and save it for a rainy day." That's what I do.'

As he expertly drove me through the city, I tried not to look disappointed that this outlook is still accepted without being questioned. I bit my tongue and continued chatting amiably all the way to my destination.

The thing is, I'm used to this outlook. It wasn't an

isolated incident. I hear this sort of thing a lot, and not just from chatty, opinionated taxi drivers.

You will already realise that I profoundly disagree with his financial attitude, but it's not so much the content of the financial advice, it's how it's perpetuated that most disappoints. I'm sure he and his grandad are lovely gentlemen, and in some ways this is why hearing this sort of thing hurts me so much.

That piece of unfortunate financial advice has already survived two generations. How many more is it going to pass through in the future? Not only that, but the taxi driver shares this sort of thinking all day, every day around one of the biggest cities in the world. It makes me wince to think of the influence it might already have had!

This is an example of financial illiteracy being passed on unquestioningly – purely saving cash is soon eroded by inflation, for example, and offers no opportunity for growth – and doing a little bit of damage everywhere it goes. Many people are brought up with the idea that investing and financial success isn't for them – it's for those who are already wealthy.

And, of course, financial literacy and money management still isn't taught in schools, so the cycle is not being broken – it's being strengthened every time this piece of homespun wisdom is shared. This is what I mean by 'the cycle', and I want to help you break it.

The fact that you're reading this book shows that you think differently from the taxi driver and his grandfather. We *can* learn to take control of our money, and not only that but learn to grow it and see financial success, no matter what our upbringing.

Facts

People who become financially successful don't have an extra piece of their brain that gives them some secret knowledge about getting rich, a financial plug-in they can use to increase their chances of becoming wealthy.

I'm sure you're thinking, 'I realise that, but they probably had a different upbringing from me. Or they came from a rich background. Or they were educated about money early on and it's too late for me to catch up now. And anyway, I just don't do money.'

This temptation to characterise financially successful people as somehow separate from the rest of us and our own opportunities and limitations in life is frustrating for a couple of reasons.

First, it's wrong. I work with many financially successful people, and they come from a huge range of different backgrounds – some monied, some not; some financially savvy themselves, some less so. They are not finance professors or investing experts – they just have, or are willing to be guided on, the principles and behaviours that underpin financial success. These ideas and activities are available to everyone.

Second, holding the view that financially successful people are in some way lucky or different absolves us from the need to take action ourselves. We can stay in the safe cocoon of inaction in a straightforward world where some people are born with the gifts to become wealthy and others simply aren't and must accept it.

If we're not financially successful, then we tend to think it's not the fault of our spending habits, our reluctance to build and stick to a financial plan or a commitment to save and invest for our financial future every month; it's the fault of the fickle financial gods, or the media, or the government – anyone but us.

For many, it's easier to avoid addressing financial behaviour and decisions because it can often mean having to address some uncomfortable truths about our lives. Ironically, many of us tend to know just enough about finance in order to put us off from delving deeper, when the reverse should actually be the case.

Finance can also be a complicated topic to just pile right into. You could read and study the *FT* (*Financial Times*, the UK's daily newspaper that looks at economics, markets and free trade) for years without necessarily having any useful or meaningful understanding of what you've read.

It's not so bad if you have an interest in numbers; you'll be better disposed to seeking out information and building up your knowledge if you enjoy it. But if it doesn't interest you – and I get that not everyone is a money geek like me – then this combination of facing up to uncomfortable truths and a complex subject matter could be pretty off-putting.

The situation you're in is that money is all around you. It is pretty much the fabric of society and influences everything from the day-to-day ebb and flow of your life to your likely lifespan. Saying you 'don't do money' and ducking out isn't just a financially suicidal way to conduct your life; it literally doesn't make sense in a society that is structured around financial fundamentals. It's like fish saying they don't do water.

We are all in this game; it is being played all around us, and if you are to create from it the best life for yourself and those you love, then you need to learn the rules and step onto the pitch. In summary, start playing it intentionally.

Solutions

When we're preparing to write or edit our own money stories, we need some guidance on how they could be different. After we've been repeating the same mantra to ourselves, for years in some cases, telling ourselves the same story over and over again, it can be difficult to climb out of this entrenched narrative and see it another way.

For each of us, the characters will be different, the ending might be happier and there are fewer twists and turns along the way. Sure, there will probably still be surprises, but they can be surprises you've also prepared for – if that's not too much of a contradiction. Learning and understanding what's possible in this new narrative are the first steps towards achieving financial success and independence.

For many of us, this means getting to grips with financial fundamentals. We need to learn a little more about how financial planning and investment works so we can get a foothold and understand what we need to do, and what we need to stop doing.

They will be the achievable, realistic components of a new and positive story that's much more likely to end in success. I don't want you to feel you haven't enough starting knowledge to read this book because that's not true. You don't need any.

Money is universal and affects us all and that's as much as you need to know. Hopefully, if I do nothing else over the next few chapters, I will give you the confidence to engage with those financial fundamentals and set you up with the tools to start building towards wealth and financial success.

I'm not going to overwhelm you with complicated theories or present a comprehensive guide to 'what finance is'. There are plenty of these books in existence already. I want to share the wisdom that's hard to google. It's not a manual for everything finance, nor an academic textbook, nor an exhaustive and meticulous set of rules.

It won't tell you everything about investing, because you don't need to know everything. I will tell you what I think you need to know to be financially successful – the essence of financial and investing success.

The problem with finance and investing information is that there is just too much of it out there, not too little. The everyday person wants less, but more focused, information that's been carefully selected to help them understand their situation more clearly. This is what I'm going to give you here.

I want to make this information as accessible as possible while still being useful, so I'm only going to give you what I think you need to know to be successful, and strip away the distractions.

Think of this information more as a very practical philosophy than a theory. It will give you the fundamental facts, the smart financial principles and the right mindset for achieving financial success – because, as you'll find out, your behaviour is actually more important and critical than the specific financial decisions you make.

You can argue about which is the best investment fund all you like, but if your financial behaviour is bad, financial success is simply never going to happen. Good financial health is not about intellect; it's about how you behave.

Everyone I have ever advised has had to learn this to some extent. They've all had to go on an educational journey, not necessarily of facts, but of behaviour, emotions and mindset. I want to give you the tools to let go of a lot of the unhelpful or incorrect assumptions and ideas you might have been carrying around with you about money until now.

To make this point more forcefully: you have the capacity to be the biggest threat to your own financial success over anything that exists out there in the world. You should not worry about market volatility and returns – you should be concentrating on maintaining your own healthy financial behaviour.

There are things to learn – from how the stock market works to how your natural human behaviour goes against your long-term financial interests – but there are things to unlearn too. And just to be clear, when you see the term 'stock market' or 'the market' I mean the place where investors buy and sell shares of companies. These shares are also known as 'stocks'. You may hear these phrases outside of this book. Ultimately the stock market is a collection of global companies and businesses that you and I use every single day.

We all fail on occasion, but carrying around failures like a badge of honour is not going to help you. Mistakes are nothing more than learning opportunities. Bad things will happen in your life at some point. It's not win or lose; it's win or learn. However, keeping a steady head and maintaining my prescribed philosophy towards money will help you live a comfortable life right through to your financial finish line.

I've been on a lifelong quest to identify the valuable essentials and strip away the unnecessary noise in achieving financial success so that it's digestible, manageable, non-daunting, approachable and accessible. This book is the result of that quest.

Meat or veg?

Let me bring to light the madness of humans in a short story.

I attended a financial adviser annual conference in Liverpool. The organisers, in their desire to have everything in place, sent a very short survey prior to the event asking the delegates if they wanted the meat or the vegetarian option for lunch. A simple question for which you'd think you could rely on the resulting data.

Here's what happened. It was a hot venue, and the morning was rather long, so at lunchtime we were all starving. From their initial question 'Meat or veg?', the organisers had an overwhelming response in favour of the vegetarian option, so planned accordingly.

But on the day, the delegates thought, 'Bugger that, I want meat', so every time a new batch of the meat lunch boxes came out, they were snatched by the nearest person.

When humans are asked for choices prior to an event, and there are two options, they'll usually choose the one that they think is better for them; at the event, their true desire takes over.

The same happens with your finances. You will have good intentions of setting up a pension, increasing your regular investment contributions, drafting a will, but in reality you take little action when it comes to it. Your current self will constantly try to wriggle out of doing anything good for your future self.

What you need to unlearn about investing and creating wealth

At first glance, being told to unlearn something does not sound like the sort of advice you want to heed. It sounds as if you're being told to forget a secret you shouldn't know or even encouraged to dumb yourself down. But be assured, this is absolutely not the case. In the world of financial advice it is crucial to your long-term financial success.

As a normal, sociable, intelligent human being, you will probably have been subjected to dozens, if not hundreds, of unhelpful, misleading or incorrect pieces of financial advice over the years. It's my job not just to make you financially informed but to strip away everything that's stopping you from achieving your full financial potential.

Learning is vital because it gives you information. Unlearning is just as crucial because it gives you wisdom. Over the following chapters I will tackle the conventional misconceptions and weed out the nonsensical, fantastic ideas that seem to have become embedded in recent thinking about personal finance.

You may believe you are doing the right thing based on what you have learned in life so far, but a lot of what you thought you knew about money will disintegrate on reading what I have to tell you. I want to change the way you think about money and set you up with a new armoury of ideas and instructions for ultimate financial success.

How to use this book

This is a handbook you can refer back to whenever you feel uncertain. Read it from front to back, then dip in and out whenever you feel you need a refresher. Let it reassure you that you're doing the right things for your family's financial future.

I'm going to take you through my key principles to give you a list of things to think about straight away. Then we'll explore debt and saving and how to take control of both of these. I'll give you practical tasks and tools that can help you, and I'll explain any unfamiliar terminology.

I'll help you to identify ways to build good behaviours and avoid some of the more common mistakes people make. I'll also point you towards where to get more help and support.

I liken good financial behaviour to looking after your physical and mental health. If you're unwell, you get a prescription. If you feel sluggish, you exercise. Money management is the same.

By the end of the book, you'll feel more confident about your finances and less afraid of investing. And remember, you're not trying to get rich for the sake of it – you're doing this to make sure you and your loved ones are comfortable.

2
Key principles

Let's get one thing out in the open before we get started. Money is dreadfully boring – and this is coming from me, a money insider and someone who lives, sleeps and breathes the money business.

However, the results of mastering money are anything but boring. Money provides financial freedom; freedom provides opportunity. The results are financial peace of mind that you can own your own home, drive a nice car and retire five years early. You'll know you will be comfortable in your retirement whatever age you stop working; be able to help your children through school/college or find somewhere to live; and buy nice gifts for family and friends.

The better educated you are about the principles of good financial behaviour, the less money you'll waste or fail to use to its full potential for you and your loved ones. Understanding money and investing is one of the greatest gifts you can give to yourself.

If you're married or in a committed relationship, please make sure to have a conversation with your partner before you decide to invest money. If you decide you'll do the investing on your own, agree beforehand how much you'll put in and where it will come from.

When it comes to risk, one partner is always more risk

averse than the other. If that's your partner, take the time to reassure them that you're not risking the next mortgage payment. If they are interested, show them where the money is, how it's growing and how it's protected.

You may choose to have two separate investment pots that you each manage as you see fit, which is great, but do still have regular conversations about how they're doing. When it comes to anything to do with money, the healthiest approach is always to be honest and talk about it.

The benefits of getting on top of your money are endless, so let's kick off with some key principles and then understand the financial stages of your life.

The six key principles

Below are my key principles to help you get your finances on track and develop healthy behaviours towards money and building wealth. Start working on them now, and you'll soon see improvement.

1. Pay off all crappy debt.
2. Take control of your expenses.
3. Insure yourself against bad health surprises.
4. Utilise tax breaks.
5. Get a pension.
6. Pay yourself first:

    » invest monthly, and the amount should feel slightly uncomfortable
    » invest in global equities
    » never react to the investment markets.

1. Pay off all crappy debt

Nothing constructive can start until your crappy debts are paid off. It's vital to remove crappy debt from your financial life before your real journey begins. Crappy debt doesn't mean your mortgage: it means your credit cards, store cards and hire purchase loans.

These debts are often created when we're young and as a result of an excessive lifestyle compared to income – keeping up with the Joneses and so on – in short, spending more than you earn. It is the sort of debt that you know you shouldn't take on even as you sign up for it.

Ideally, you need to clear these crappy debts before you start making proper financial plans for the future. At certain points in your life, credit cards and loans can be useful, practical solutions to life events and valid financial demands, but it's important to know the difference between these and impulse luxury purchases.

So, my first prescription towards financial fitness is to pay off all your crappy debt. This will also eliminate throwing good money after bad in the form of interest. Rather than another night out this month, put that money towards paying off money you already owe.

Before you add more crappy debt to your tab, ask yourself what value that purchase will be to you in the long run. In five years' time, will it have moved you any nearer to achieving financial security? Stop living beyond your means and shed these poor financial habits, buying things you don't need, with money you don't have to impress people you don't like.

If you have cleared all your crappy debt, then congratulations, you've completed step one on the journey.

2. Take control of your expenses

As boring as it is, you need to get a grasp of what you're spending: fixed monthly costs (eg mortgage/rent, utility bills, food) and discretionary costs (gym membership, restaurant bills, holidays).

Keeping a tight grip on what you spend has a far greater impact on your long-term financial health than most people realise – it's as important to determining your future financial success as the return you get from your investment portfolio over the long term (we'll come to investing in Chapter 4).

The task of totting up where your money is going each month shouldn't take you longer than 30 minutes to get a high-level overview. Then you can see what you must spend and what you can cut back on to pay down debt or put towards your future self.

3. Insure yourself against bad health surprises

Make sure you have the right amount of 'human' insurance to protect yourself and anyone financially dependent on you in the event of illness or early death. This means income protection, critical illness and life insurance cover for the income producers in the family. All forms of health insurance are designed to replace income in the event of a bad health surprise. Even life insurance in essence replaces income that has now been lost by the surviving family. (I'll come back to these in more detail in Chapter 3.)

4. Utilise tax breaks

I told you at the beginning of the chapter that money is dreadfully boring – well, tax is worse. However, it's something you need to get your head around. As your wealth increases, the tax system becomes more complex and restrictive, presenting numerous challenges and potential obstacles.

Fortunately, there are some simple wins when it comes to investing. In the UK, it's essential to understand the power of tax-efficient investment accounts, often referred to as 'tax wrappers', such as ISAs (individual savings accounts) and pensions.

These tax wrappers are designed to protect your investments from certain taxes, allowing your money to grow more effectively over time. For the majority of people, and especially for couples, these two types of accounts – ISAs and pensions – are all you really need to achieve your long-term financial goals.

They offer generous allowances and benefits that make them sufficient for most people. While these options are specific to the UK, similar tax-efficient accounts are available in many countries around the world, tailored to their respective tax systems.

By focusing on these straightforward and highly effective accounts, you can simplify your financial planning and maximise the potential of your investments. Being aware of the tax breaks available to you is vital to stop your hard-earned money being unnecessarily eroded by tax.

5. Get a pension

Unless you can live on the modest government pension, which itself is being squeezed and pressured from every angle with each year that passes, you'll need to make your own additional pension arrangements to supplement it.

If you're an employee of a company that offers to match your pension contributions, take advantage of this generous opportunity to build wealth with the free money that's on offer. If you are self-employed like me, you should assign money to pay into your own pension. I'll discuss pensions in detail in Chapter 3.

6. Pay yourself first

A tried and tested way to achieve financial freedom is through investing every single month in the right investment funds, buying regularly and allowing the investment markets to perform over time. I'll expand on this much more in Chapter 4.

The key principle to understand now is that, once you've eliminated your crappy debt, you need a fixed monthly contribution being directed towards investing for your future self.

You could achieve financial success by selling a business or inheriting money, but if this is not an option for you, the only other viable option to build wealth is by investing regularly – starting a behaviour that you can stick to and that produces financial results. I'm not talking about saving money in a bank account or having cash in an emergency fund – and certainly not about keeping it in a shoebox. I'm talking about investing in the stock market for superior returns in the long run.

The two financial stages of life: saving and spending

When it comes to your financial planning, you have to think of your life as having two distinct stages where you have to think about money. Typically, life comes in three stages: our education years, 0–20 years old; work years, 20–67; and retirement years, 68–90+. Obviously, these are broad-brush examples – people don't fall neatly into them.

The stages you need to be concerned with for your financial planning are your working years and then your retirement years. Rather than thinking of these stages as 'working' and 'retirement', it's better to apply action titles, so I call them the 'saving' and 'spending' stages. It could not be simpler:

- £ For the saving stage, as the name implies, it's clear what you need to be doing: saving and investing money every month.
- £ Your spending stage is when you spend down the assets you've accumulated.

So, the name of the game is to build up enough financial capital while you're working (saving stage) so that when you decide to stop working you'll never run out of money during your retirement (spending stage).

If you book an appointment with a typical financial adviser and they are talking you through your financial plan, you might hear them talking about your 'accumulation stage' and your 'decumulation stage' of life. In plain English, these are the saving stage and the spending stage.

When we look closer at how our lives break down like this, we can see that humans don't actually have that long to behave themselves into wealth. Most people aren't ready to start their investing journey until their thirties (if they're lucky – with the increasing unattainability of their first property, this is steadily getting later and later).

But there will come a point – hopefully sooner rather than later – when starting to save becomes a priority. From then on until the day you retire is what I call your wealth window, and it's the most important part of your saving stage – the period when all the hard work and preparation for the future is done.

How wide is this wealth creation window? Let's assume that for most people it starts slowly between the ages of 30 and 40, then ramps up between 40 and 50 and then (ideally) really gains momentum from age 50 onwards.

Once you start investing, you ideally should know (or

be told) exactly how many months you have left. Let's say you're 50 and you wanted to retire (stop working) at 60, then you have 120 months left (10 years × 12 months = 120), so you have 120 payslips to get your plan to work – see the diagram in Figure 1.

So the real wealth creation window runs for approximately 15 to 25 years, all going well. If you're a fortunate human without much financial baggage, this window would seem long enough to create real wealth, as long as you focus on behaving yourself into riches and not misbehaving your way to poverty.

Getting over the financial finish line

For me, a part of helping people to see themselves as financially self-aware beings is helping them to define what financial success means to them. That is genuinely different for all of us, but the ways of getting there are mostly the same.

In short, financial success means comfortably getting over the financial finish line: your money outlives you. Financial risk is being destitute in your old age and having to ask for handouts from your family or the state.

It's easy to make the mistake of thinking that financial success is about speedboats, tax havens and mahogany tans when it's actually much more simple, personal and achievable than that. Reaching this finish line successfully means putting enough aside when you're in the saving stage of your life so that you've enough when you reach the spending stage and maybe some left over for the next generation. You can dress it up and add your goals to tick off your bucket list and so forth, but the basic idea is the same.

Key principles

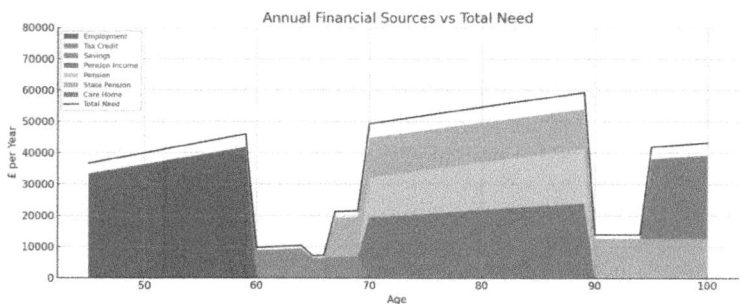

Figure 1: Annual financial sources vs total need

Now you understand the key principles, let's begin taking control.

3

Taking control

How information is presented and perceived

Being aware of how we see the world is vital in our multimedia environment, and nowhere more so than in financial advice. This is an area in which a financial adviser can provide clarity.

Framing the decision the right way can make a significant difference to the way you view your financial life and your relationship with your financial decisions. For instance, you might have the impression that investing in the stock market is a risk. If you reframe it to think of the market as a collection of the best-performing businesses in the world, you can see that it would make sense to buy shares in these profitable organisations. A financial adviser can help you to consider your options and make financially healthy investment decisions.

So, it's important to frame your financial decisions positively and practically to enable you to make the right ones, and in a timely manner, today. Taking financial advice and becoming financially informed gives you the tools to start building this new money story for yourself.

Your questions relating to this money story might be:

- £ How is the narrative going to play out?
- £ What are the chapters going to look like?
- £ What are the big questions I need to answer?

The big questions are pretty much the same for all of us:

- £ Am I going to be financially secure in the future?
- £ When can I retire?
- £ Is my family going to be well provided for as I get older and after I'm gone?

These are the considerations that will mould your story. You might lose sight of them among the short-term and immediate concerns of the everyday, but you need to keep them front and centre at all times. They aren't just a part of the story – they *are* the story.

Answers to these questions will emerge over your lifetime. They will be answered whether you like it or not, so you have a choice. You can either sit back and let life provide the answers and hope that this matches your plans, or you can take control and decide the answers, which will be crucial parts of your story.

By seeking financial advice you're also, in a way, asking another question: what financial mistakes am I making? Sometimes I will meet with a client who has written what they think is part of their story and they may need me to just add in an element of their choosing. They might ask for a specific pension product or tell me they want to invest in a new portfolio they've heard about from their work colleagues. Or they have decided that clearing their mortgage is the best way forward for them and their family and that this is their priority over everything else. In some cases they might be right, but it's my job to look at the big picture, to remind them of the entire narrative of their story and keep them on track for financial success.

Anyone can take control of their money, and that includes you. It starts when you want to learn – you have to be a grown-up and take charge. You have to arrange the cards you've been dealt, take unconditional ownership of your situation and plan your way forward.

It'll take a lot of work – why should it be easy? – and you'll need to adjust your behaviour and mindset along the way, but this can all be done little by little.

Take the first steps

Believe it or not, the key to achieving financial success is simply to start by taking small, consistent steps, little by little. It might feel overwhelming at first, but the hardest part is to readjust your mindset, tackle the key principles set out in Chapter 2 and embrace the healthier behaviour of stashing money, first to clear debts and then to make it work towards your future.

Once you get going with the basics and can begin investing, increasing your contributions over time will feel much easier. When I talk about investing, I'm specifically referring to the stock market – particularly global equity funds.

By starting to invest in these funds, not only do you begin to build your financial future, but you also gain hands-on experience and a better understanding of how the stock market works and what the journey of investing feels like. I will discuss these funds in more depth in Chapter 4.

Most people think they're not yet rich enough to start investing or planning their financial future, and so they stay in the zone of inaction. They're waiting for conditions to be perfect: being in their ideal job, being paid a perfect amount, moving to that perfect place.

You'll never achieve perfection – you've got to be

happy to start to change your behaviour when things are a little scrappy. Stop waiting, get going and tweak later. Your behaviour is everything in the wealth creation game – information and knowledge mean absolutely nothing without behaviour change.

Every time someone asks me when they should start investing and how much, my answers are always yesterday and more than you think. This is because my answers are not about financial advantage, they're about behaviour. So, trust me: the most important thing is to start, and start today.

Stop craving shiny, useless things

In today's affluent consumer economy, a clear trend emerges: as income rises, particularly beyond the level required to meet basic needs, spending on luxury items increases. These luxury goods often fulfil wants rather than necessities, catering more to desires than essential needs. Eventually, most people reach a point where these shiny, useless things lose their appeal. This realisation varies in timing for each individual; some may never outgrow the urge to accumulate.

Typically, I've found that younger people are more attracted to these items. As people age and gain wisdom, they often find deeper meaning within themselves, beyond material possessions. To quote Tyler Durden in the film *Fight Club*, 'The things you own end up owning you.' Never forget what Tyler said.

From a financial planning perspective, curbing the urge to buy shiny, useless things can have a profound impact. It not only reduces discretionary spending (see key principle 2: take control of your expenses), but also allows for better investment of capital – you invest this money in your future self (key principle 6: pay yourself first) rather than spending it on something that will depreciate in value.

Calculate how much you'll need to retire on

If a financial adviser asks you 'What's your number?', they're not looking to give you a call. In our world this means, 'Have you calculated the amount you'll need to comfortably live on for the rest of your life?'

The point at which you amass this amount is effectively when you get to retire, or work becomes optional. For many of us – living our daily lives, going about our business – we have an idea that we will retire at some point in the future and that to some degree we are saving towards it with a pension or maybe investments, but it remains vague. It's something that might look a long way off, too far off to think about yet as it's at some undefined point in the future. Taking the time now to work out how much you'll need to retire on sharpens up your focus on the future and gives you a goal to aim for, starting from today.

Your 'number' applies only to you and depends on your lifestyle, family and future. At first, this exercise can feel like a daunting prospect. For the uninitiated, setting out to calculate the stark reality of an actual financial figure can seem alarming compared with the false comfort of blissful ignorance. But trust me, this usually gives way to relief and satisfaction once the process has been carried out.

Put simply, the way you work out the number is to calculate how much it would cost you to live your ideal life every year and project this into the future, taking into account the key possibilities and life events along the way as well as the effects of inflation. This gives you a target financial figure and an estimated date of retirement.

Knowing your number gives you clarity on your financial path and genuine comfort that you've worked out exactly what you'll need to save and aim for, so all you have to do is follow your financial plan towards it. It empowers you and puts you in control of your money, rather than the reverse. This is good financial behaviour and a mature approach to your financial wellbeing.

Good behaviour supports more good behaviour as, once you know your number and when you can retire, it can be a great way to keep you motivated and committed to your financial plan as you move towards it. It's so much easier to resist the temptations of today when you have a clear view of the rewards of tomorrow.

When you get to retirement, you will no longer be earning. Instead, you will be relying on whatever pension pots you have, plus any money from investments. When you're investing now, you're making sure you have enough to live on later.

It varies from person to person, but if you have a rough idea of how much your future (in retirement) monthly spending will be, you can work out how much you need to invest. I use the term 'your number' to represent that personal amount.

The key aspect in working out your number is to first agree what your likely monthly spending will be. Once you have this you can then proceed to work out your approximate number target.

Let's say that you think you'll spend £1,000 per month when you reach retirement age. An easy way to roughly calculate how much invested capital you'll need in order for that to happen is by using the 4 per cent rule.

Simply put, if you're investing wisely, it suggests you can safely withdraw around 4 per cent of your portfolio each year without running out of money. To work out how much capital you'll need in order to sustain your monthly spending level for 30 years (from the day you start retirement to the end of your life), multiply monthly spending by 300.

Where do we get the 300 from? Well, 12 months × 25 = 300, divided by 0.04 (4 per cent) is 25. Multiplying your monthly need by 300 gives the same result as multiplying your annual need by 25.

Examples

This method gives you a quick, back-of-the-envelope way to check how close you are to financial independence:

- £ monthly spending £1k × 300 = you need £300k (in your investment pots by the time you retire)
- £ monthly spending £3k × 300 = you need £900k (in your investment pots by the time you retire)
- £ monthly spending £5k × 300 = you need £1.5m (in your investment pots by the time you retire).

This is based on the assumption that you're withdrawing 4 per cent of your capital each year.

If you wish to be more cautious, you can multiply by 350. Here are some examples:

- £ monthly spending £1k × 350 = you need £350k (in your investment pots by the time you retire)
- £ monthly spending £3k × 350 = you need £1,050,000 (in your investment pots by the time you retire)
- £ monthly spending £5k × 350 = you need £1,750,000 (in your investment pots by the time you retire).

This is meant to be a very loose guide, so don't get too caught up in the specifics. There are countless ways to measure and interpret this, and people often debate the best approach. While it may not be perfect, it's a decent method to get you started. (To find out more about the 4 per cent rule go to Investopedia – see the link in the References at the back of the book.)

So, take it with a pinch of salt, relax and make a start on some sums. Remember, it's just a tool to give you some perspective. You will be refining it through your financial plan over the coming years.

Create and maintain a financial plan

To achieve good financial health, you need to have a financial life plan. This is vital because it takes stock of where you are today versus where you want to be, and makes sure you square the two things up. Think of it as bringing your future life into the present so you can do something positive about it now.

As a professional financial plan builder, I know the benefits of creating financial life plans. I've created hundreds of plans for clients and, more importantly, I've also *updated* hundreds of plans. It's a pleasure to create the first financial plan for a family – listing all their goals and what they wish to achieve, with money being the facilitator of these goals. Your plan should list everything that requires time, money and preparation in order to achieve it.

The initial plan is not the important element of the process – it's the planning process that's crucial. The initial plan will lay the foundations, but financial plans are built to be fluid, reflecting life – a rigid plan is not a realistic plan.

The real value is created by frequently coming back to your plan (at least annually) and making the changes that become necessary as life plays out. The plan itself reflects just one period of time – the planning process trumps the actual plan.

Life is full of surprises, and will test your ability to stay committed to your carefully thought-out financial plan. I know from experience that it's hard to stick to an agreed plan without having a caring adviser in your corner – somebody to hold you to account and be a sounding board for major decisions.

It's also important to have somebody who can identify any financial misbehaviour and ensure there are no gaps in your plan – you can't see your own blind spots. Making a financial plan together with a financial adviser gives you the confidence that you're on the right track and you're doing the right things, and avoids the paralysis of doing nothing because you are fearful of making a mistake. You can find more details on working with a financial adviser in Chapter 5.

As you will learn in Chapter 4, the fifth of my ten financial commandments states that having an investment portfolio is not the same as having a financial plan. Many ill-informed investors make this mistake. The mistake can be dangerous, because those making it think they're doing everything they need to do to be financially successful. They think they're good with money, that they're doing all they can to make their financial future secure. They're certainly moving in the right direction, but a portfolio is by no means the whole story, both in terms of the comprehensive approach to finances that's required and the behavioural mindset needed.

Investors who fail to reach their financial goals are the ones who are forever focused on a portfolio and the markets, because this leads to bad decisions. Investors who succeed are the ones who are always focused on their financial plan. It is the most important element for you to concentrate on and get right.

What a good financial plan should contain

This is a basic list for what your good financial plan should contain:

- £ your monthly income
- £ your monthly outgoings
    - » fixed costs such as utility bills
    - » mortgage/rent
    - » loan repayments
    - » insurance policy payments
- £ pension contributions and employer matched contributions
- £ potential pay increases or bonuses
- £ savings accounts (including to an emergency fund if you have one)
- £ sundries/luxuries
- £ investment contributions
- £ potential one-off costs (a big holiday, car repairs)
- £ other debt repayments.

It should also take account of:

- £ all of the people involved
- £ spending patterns throughout your life – aka your personal burn rate: how much you'll be spending each month
- £ all the income received throughout life
- £ what you have accumulated already – your savings, your investment, your pensions
- £ other significant assets that you own
- £ inflation and investment assumptions
- £ debts
- £ insurance
- £ all of your key life events – transitions from one

phase of your life to another (earning to spending/retirement), goals and aspirations
- £ a comprehensive timeline for the future, including all the above.

It's important to think of your financial plan as a fluid process and journey, not a rigid destination. The plan will help you to monitor whether you are on track to achieve your financial life goals – your financial finish line – and, if not, indicate how and where you can make changes to ensure you are on course to meet your targets.

If you're off track, you will need to trigger some financial levers to ensure your plan will be successful.

Building wealth for the unknowns

In my work with clients, I have built hundreds of financial plans for families. These plans include all the knowns and some 'known unknowns'. There is also provision for essential and non-essential items, an allocation for possible medical expenses and aspirational bucket-list expenses. However, as we know, 'Man plans, and God laughs.' One thing missing from these plans is the 'unknown unknowns'. By their very nature, these cannot be planned for – or can they?

Having seen people's lives unfold and personally witnessed their investment journeys, I've concluded that curtailing people's investment returns because they are already projected to get over the financial finish line is short sighted.

Knowing that unknown financial shocks can hit you out of the blue, creating additional wealth can only give you more freedom and opportunity. The stock market is the perfect vehicle for insuring against life's 'unknown unknowns'. It's a powerful and lucrative force that can protect you financially from life's 'unknowns'.

One of the biggest 'unknowns' I've seen is parents supporting adult children in divorce. This trend is not going anywhere. Another example is unexpected health issues that require more money than the financial plan predicted.

While traditional financial plans aim to meet specific goals, it's crucial to save and invest beyond your immediate and expected needs. You must consider the potential challenges you may face down the road.

Life rarely unfolds as we envision, and building a margin of safety into your financial planning is one way of countering the fragility of your plans. This extra wealth can serve as a safety net when unforeseen circumstances arise, providing security and confidence in the face of the unknown. If this extra wealth is not needed during your lifetime, more wealth will be available to benefit your family or worthy causes.

Deploy financial levers

To successfully cross your financial finish line, you have to understand the financial levers you may need to pull to get you there. Some are working for you and some against you, and you have varying levels of control over all of them. Starting with the most important, these are:

- £ die sooner
- £ spend less
- £ earn more
- £ work longer
- £ invest more
- £ get a better investment return
- £ receive a large capital inflow (eg business sale, inheritance)
- £ rightsize/downsize your main home
- £ release equity from your home
- £ a combination of the above.

Die sooner

One simple way to ensure you cross the financial finish line is to die sooner. This means you wouldn't need your money to last to my default assumption age of 100. When I say this to my clients, there's always a little chuckle, but it helps them see instantly and clearly what their financial plan is for.

In financial planning, this is a lever you can't control. Certain lifestyle activities and hereditary diseases may shorten your life expectancy, but it's always wiser to plan for a long life than to take a gamble and end up with too much life left at the end of your money.

Spend less

Controlling your spending can have a huge impact on your long-term financial health, but many of us find it one of the most difficult levers to master. Its importance cannot be understated, however, as it will have such a huge impact on your family's finances.

You have significant control over this and need the self-discipline to achieve it well. Be mindful of your daily, weekly and monthly spending, think carefully about whether you need that new car, avoid lifestyle creep and marshal your expenditure with a quarterly check-in, ideally diarised so it'll happen. Becoming more aware of where your money goes is vital.

For example, if your net income every month is £3,000 and your monthly lifestyle costs are £3,000, you're spending everything you have coming in, so you have no spare, or what I like to call 'breakout', income.

If, however, you restrict your lifestyle expenses to £2,000 per month, then you have created £1,000 in breakout income. In these circumstances, you can pay your future self with it by investing the whole sum rather than splurging it on a holiday or new Xbox – consider a three-star hotel instead of that five-star you love so much! This is a sign of money maturity – seeking to create breakout income and then using it to build a healthy financial future for yourself and your family.

When I started my first job at 22, my monthly pay was £700 after tax. Having just left university, this was a huge leap in income, and I felt richer than I had ever been, but in a short space of time my life expenses started to creep up and keep pace with my new income.

Then, when I moved to a new job, my take-home pay went up to £1,000 after tax and I thought I'd have a spare £300 in my bank account every month. Soon enough, my lifestyle crept up again to claim this additional cash.

The moral of the story is to be aware of this lifestyle creep and to take action to stop it expanding to hoover up all your available income every month. You need to think again of your future self. Paying your future self should be your biggest monthly outgoing and everything else should come after this. It's not an easy thing to do to start with, but it's an extremely effective and powerful habit to get into for your future financial health.

Earn more or work longer

We have some level of control over how much we earn, within the boundaries of our career and abilities. If earning more creates more resources for you to direct towards your future financial security – and not towards a more extravagant lifestyle today – then this can be a powerful lever to propel you in the direction you need to go. Additionally, if you love your job or just feel you could continue past the traditional retirement age, this can have a really positive effect on your long-term prosperity.

From a financial point of view, in most cases pay rises are detrimental to your long-term financial plan. As you'll now start spending more, the amount you need to save for your future has also increased. If instead you save more than half the new income, then it will be beneficial for your future self.

Invest more

Spending less and earning more are solid behaviours in themselves, but you need to use the extra money you generate wisely for it to bear fruit for you. Think of investing as deferred spending. What you don't spend today, if you invest it, goes towards making you more comfortable tomorrow. It's that simple.

Another useful way to think of it is paying your future self first, which I covered briefly in Chapter 2. Once you make that clear connection and understand that this money is all coming back to you, you're far more likely to be able to increase your investing.

When you first joined the workforce, you had an abundance of human capital, which was your ability to earn an income for years into the future, but probably little investment capital to invest. You may have had student debt, and your initial income was likely to have been low, but you had your whole future ahead of you and time to fix the problem. As the years go by, you should aim to exchange your human capital for investment capital, which means converting your efforts in the workplace into investable assets for your future security.

You're never ever going to save and invest too much – it's impossible. Work out what percentage of your net income you're saving and investing and always be looking for ways you can increase this year on year.

Being aware of how much you are investing as a

percentage of your monthly income is vital (the overall figure should include saving, investments and both your and your employer's contributions to your pension). Everyone should know it and keep it in their head at all times. I often think I should blow it up in big numbers and project it onto the wall of my office for each client, so they're confronted with the reality every time we meet.

The question is, what percentage should you be saving/investing? I don't like to operate using strict rules because we're all different, but if you pushed me on this I'd say that as a minimum you should be aiming to invest 20 per cent of your net income.

Anything under 5 per cent is insufficient. More than 5 per cent is some concession to making an effort. Above 10 per cent shows decent willingness and over 15 per cent is when you're gathering some serious momentum.

From 20 per cent onwards is when things start to happen. When planning ahead with clients, I can show them that this will have a material effect on their future financial wellbeing. It is the amount you need to invest to start making a real impact.

When my clients get up to this number and beyond, I can see that they are taking things seriously, they're listening to the needs of their future financial selves and not blocking them out with the noise and temptations of the present day. This is all about behaviour and control. We are bombarded at every turn with inducements to part with our money today; it's just the way society works. It's just the way humans work.

You can't just blame this unquenchable thirst to consume on advertising, the demands of your family or on the economy and rising cost of living. You are the agent of your own destiny, and *you* make the decisions on how much you decide to spend and therefore how much you decide not to save. Increasing your investing percentage means spending less and saving more. It's simple, but not easy.

The greater the percentage you invest, the more fulfilling a life you're going to have in the future and the sooner you'll get there. Investing will create your future freedom.

Once you start to see the saving versus spending proportions as two sides of the same coin, you'll start to understand how they interact with each other and how controlling them quickly affects your prosperity.

For example, as you increase your investing percentage, you correspondingly decrease your lifestyle spending. Everything is accelerated because you're building up your future retirement money while also closely controlling and reducing your monthly expenditure so your money will go even further. It's a double whammy and a double positive impact.

It's important to note here that this isn't about how much you earn or the size of your salary relative to anyone else. This bit isn't important. To put it another way, your future self doesn't care what you earn; your future self only cares about the proportion of what you earn that you're investing.

The financial amounts you earn or save don't matter in themselves, but the percentages do. It's about your behaviour with money rather than the money itself. Once you have enough investment capital that you can comfortably live off for the rest of your life, you're what I call 'financially independent': you're not dependent on a wage or anyone else for your financial survival – the position we're all striving for.

It's also important not to underestimate the value of your human capital at the start of your career. It may be invisible but it's real.

Get a better investment return

Achieving a better return on your investments than you're currently getting could be a very impactful lever, but not as powerful as many people think. It admittedly has a bigger impact the longer the timespan over which you're investing, but it isn't anywhere near as significant as the levers I have listed already. To find out how long you'll be investing for, assume you will live a long life and subtract your age from 100. Just because you stop working doesn't mean you stop investing; keeping your money outpacing inflation is the target.

It's understandable why so many people think investment return is fundamentally important in their future success: because it doesn't involve them having to modify their own behaviour or delay their gratification for a shiny, new thing a few years into the future. It's a painless security blanket to cling to when they don't want to face up to their financial reality.

Receive a large capital inflow (breakout cash)

Breakout cash is a similar concept to the breakout income (see 'Spend less' above), but is generated by selling assets such as a business or a property, or it could come from an inheritance – these are the main three sources. However, receiving a large capital inflow is not something that everyone can benefit from. They may have no assets that they can sell and would not be receiving an inheritance.

If the nature of your personal and work life is that you're never going to have breakout cash – no business or assets to sell, and no rich elderly relatives – then your only option to create wealth is to focus on your breakout income and spend less money on creature comforts.

Rightsize/downsize

Many of my clients, usually at a later stage of their lives, decide to sell the main home they've lived in for many years and move to usually a smaller/cheaper property. When they do this, they usually receive a large cash inflow from the difference in price from selling one house and buying a smaller one – for example, selling a house for £500k and buying a smaller place for £300k. After some buying, selling and moving costs, you've cleared a chunk of cash that, as above, you can choose to invest or save.

To be clear, the terms 'rightsize' and 'downsize' in this sense refer to moving into a home of an appropriate size for the stage of life you're in. When the kids move out, if you have them, you probably don't need so many bedrooms, so you find somewhere that's the right size for you.

Release equity from your home

Another option for people who've used up all their cash is to withdraw cash from the home that they live in. It's usually the last resort, but a really good one nonetheless. You should think of an equity release mortgage as a secured overdraft against your house. You can either receive a lump sum, eg £50k, or you can opt for an 'income', such as £2k per month forever. The plans are very flexible these days.

The 'only' catch is that the money you borrow, whether that's income payments or a lump sum, has interest added to the total, and the interest compounds each year that you owe the mortgage lender the money.

Take out human insurance

You saw in Chapter 2 that one of my key principles is to insure yourself. This is the insurance you need to protect you and your loved ones against the nasty surprises that life could throw at you. It's often called 'protection' but, to make clear what it is and what it's protecting, I like to rename it 'human insurance'.

I want to be clear that I personally hope that every penny you spend on human insurance is a complete waste of money. I love making my contribution to my insurance policies every single month. It sounds counterintuitive, but it just means that I'm fit and healthy and with no need to make a claim. Any claim on it means I'm ill, incapacitated or 6ft under. When it comes to insurance, we often insure the golden eggs but we don't insure the golden goose.

By this, I mean that we regularly take out insurance for our phones, cars, possessions, homes, holidays, but these are all the golden eggs. Often you will find an individual is paying out to four or five different insurance policies for these every single month but none to protect themselves, the golden goose.

If they die, become ill or get hit by a bus, then no insurance policy will pay out to support them or their dependants. This is worrying. It's a serious gap in their protection plan, and one that needs to be filled. Insuring yourself is vital.

The three types of insurance you need to know about are life insurance, critical illness cover and income protection. These types of insurance are all ultimately intended to replace income:

Life insurance replaces the income of the dead person whose 'income' will be missed by their spouse/partner/children.

Critical illness replaces the 'income' of the person who's still alive but not working due to a serious illness and therefore no income is coming in.

Income protection provides a monthly 'income' to someone alive who's experienced an event that has resulted in them now not being able to work and receive an income.

Life insurance

Who needs life cover? The simple answer is that you need life cover if, when you die, you would leave a liability or dependants. This could be a debt that needs to be serviced, like a mortgage, or children or a spouse who depend on your income to live their lives.

If you're single with no spouse or children you don't technically need to take out life insurance. You might still want to, to give those you leave behind a better inheritance in terms of a larger estate, but this is a discretionary choice. However, if you have dependants and a mortgage or debt, I would say that taking out life insurance is essential. The life insurance market is huge and there are many options to consider, but you only need to know the high-level information.

There are two types of life cover. First, there's the type that pays out a clearly defined lump sum, let's say £500k, and spans a fixed period. If you are 40 years old and you take out a life insurance policy for 20 years, whether you make a claim on it in year one or in year 19, the policy would pay out the same amount of £500k. This is called a level term policy – the payout amount will always stay the same, as will the monthly premiums.

There is also the option of taking out a decreasing term policy. Using the same figures, this means the policy will pay out £500k in the first year but the payout amount will decrease on a sliding scale over the 20-year period down to zero at the end. This is a cheaper policy and is usually taken out to cover a debt, such as a mortgage, that is itself steadily decreasing.

The second type of life insurance is an income death policy, also known as a family income benefit policy. This is an income policy payable on death, but the payment does not come in a lump sum. It would be broken down into, for example, an annual payment of £30k per year for the remainder of the policy.

For the same 20-year period, if the policyholder died in year one, their loved ones would receive an annual income for the remaining 19 years of £30k per year. If they died in year ten, the family would receive £30k per year for the remaining ten years of the policy. The good thing about family income benefit is that the potential payout is very large, and the payments are very reasonable. It's a very useful life insurance policy but is often overlooked as an option.

A final option to discuss here is something called index-linked. This basically means both the policy amount and the monthly contributions can be linked to some form of inflation (rising prices) – long story short, in most cases it's worth adding this to your plans, as this way your policy maintains its value. But, as they say, exceptions may apply.

Critical illness cover

Insurance companies list the conditions that qualify for critical illness cover, with each usually offering the capacity to add further conditions to that list for individuals to insure themselves against. The main illnesses are cancer, heart attack and stroke.

As an example of how critical illness cover works, a 40-year-old taking out a critical illness policy for £100k over 20 years would be paid that as a lump sum if they suffered one of those illnesses within that period.

Critical illness insurance is very expensive, about five to seven times more expensive than life insurance. This is because the chances of having a critical illness and surviving are far higher than the chances of unexpectedly dying.

Life insurance has generally been getting cheaper over the decades as people are living for longer. It's possible to combine the two and take out a life insurance policy and a critical illness policy to insure against both.

Income protection

This is absolutely crucial. I believe anyone with a job needs to take out an income protection policy. You should think of this as disaster insurance. It's not for a twisted ankle on the squash court, or other common problems. It means serious illness and incapacity and not being able to work for a number of years.

As an example, a 40-year-old earning £100k per year who wants to protect their income to some degree could take out a policy for £30k. If they were to get hit by a bus, the policy would then pay out £30k a year, potentially tax-free, usually until the date of retirement. Hence, your income is replaced.

Remember – make sure you are insuring the golden goose, not *only* the golden eggs!

Stash some FU money

What is FU money? I'm sure you can guess what the initials stand for! It's a way of thinking – a movement even – that encourages people to build up a sum of money that would allow them some financial freedom.

There's some debate over exactly how much financial freedom this means. There are those who think it means the ability to literally say 'FU' to their boss and the nine-to-five routine and walk off into the sunset, never to set their alarm clock again. This would be full-blown financial independence, but I don't personally define FU money this way.

I take it to exist somewhere in between an emergency fund and an amount that would allow you some wiggle room. It's perhaps as much a springboard as a safety net. So, if your boss is making unreasonable demands one day, you can have a frank exchange of views, leave the job and then spend some time working out what direction you'll take next.

It allows you to loosen the shackles and create for yourself a space where you can take stock and consider your options for a while, and still keep up the mortgage payments and looking after your family. The amount you build up will depend on all the moving parts in your life, but it can be a tremendous benefit for your wellbeing knowing that you have options, and a buffer between you and skid row.

If you actually sit down and take two minutes to work out what the amount might be to keep you afloat for maybe six months without any income, you will be genuinely surprised. And when you weigh this up against the peace of mind you'd get knowing you have this option in your back pocket it often becomes a no-brainer to begin work on building it up. The reason I love the concept of FU money is because it can be the first step you take towards controlling your money and making it work for you, and not the other way round.

You're using money to create some freedom for yourself, increase your independence and give yourself more control over your existence, which is exactly what money should be used for. So, keeping one eye on the key principles, once you've paid off all crappy debt, make a start on stashing away some FU money, utilising your tax breaks.

Start investing today – don't waste time creating an emergency fund

If you pick up a 'basic guide to personal finance' book or google the steps you need to take to get on the road to wealth, most will say something like: get out of debt; build an emergency fund; start investing. In that order. It makes complete logical and economic sense to follow these three steps.

However, what I have found in many years of dealing with humans is that life can often get in the way of logic and economic sense. If we tell people they can only ever start investing once they have successfully built up an emergency fund of perhaps three months' worth of living expenses, what if they never get past this point? What if they find it so difficult to build this safety nest egg that they never start investing, even the smallest of amounts, to start building financial security for their future?

Other advisers may argue against this and insist these three steps must be followed in the correct order and that it's irresponsible to do it any other way, but I don't agree. If you've been chasing your tail trying to build up this amount for years and got nowhere, it's time to take a more human perspective on the situation and put in a pragmatic solution.

Getting into the mindset and habit of investing each and every month and putting money aside to grow for the future is absolutely crucial, even if it needs to happen before or at least concurrently with a drive to pull together your emergency fund of cash for a rainy day or your FU money. You might turn round one day to find that you've been scrabbling towards this emergency fund for 20 years, losing out on two decades' worth of investment growth and still no nearer to your goals.

Think of it as paying your future self first and getting your money to work harder for you. It's not irresponsible, as some financial advice would have you believe; it's just a human and pragmatic approach to your financial future.

Make sure you're in your workplace pension

One of the key principles of good financial behaviour is to get a workplace pension – if you're employed by a company that offers these.

If you're self-employed like me/run your own business, you also need to set one up, but all of the contributions will come from you and you won't get the extra contributions that an employer would pay in on your behalf. There are various schemes you can sign up for online, and you can manage most of them directly from an app. Ask trusted peers for recommendations and do your due diligence to choose which one is right for you.

The pensions offered to most employees by employers are superb. The travesty is that a lot of employees don't maximise their pensions at work because they don't understand their options and they're unschooled about investing.

I have to say this again, most employees woefully underutilise their workplace pension scheme, so don't let that be you.

This is such a risk in today's climate. The pension age is being increased in the UK and the amount your employer can contribute is declining with each passing year. You can't assume that your state pension will be enough on its own. And this applies whether you're an employee or self-employed – you need your own pension fund.

It is compulsory in the UK for every employer to offer

a workplace pension scheme, and you are automatically enrolled when you start to work for them. They must pay minimum monthly contributions for you. There are some exceptions, relating to how much you earn. (Learn more at gov.uk – see References for the full details.)

One of the most important parts of a workplace pension for employees is the maximum matched contribution (MMC), so let's dig into that now. Lots of employers offer an MMC. These work on a matched contribution basis, and understanding them is crucial. In a typical workplace pension, it works like this. If you pay a percentage of your salary into your pension fund then your employer will contribute too, typically with the same amount. This could be as high as 10 per cent (and sometimes even higher), so it's worthwhile checking the maximum your employer is willing to match.

Let's take a simplistic example. You choose to pay/invest 5 per cent of your annual salary, which for this example we'll say is £125 per month, then your employer 'matches' this contribution to the tune of £125. That's £250 into your pension pot per month. You need to find out the maximum matched contribution amount available to you. It's usually between 5 per cent and 10 per cent, although it could be higher, depending on the scheme your employer uses.

This is essentially a free lunch, and billions of pounds are not being taken up by employees because they don't understand this. Broadly speaking, if you decided not to invest the 10 per cent into your pension and take it out as salary, you'll end up with around 6–8 per cent of it because income tax will be applied.

So, contact your pension team at work to find out the details of your MMC, and enjoy the additional free money from your employer. As a bonus, you can invest way more than the MMC, because you're not restricted by it. You could invest 15 per cent, even if the MMC is only 10 per cent. What I'm saying is: don't be restricted by whatever the MMC percentage is, but certainly utilise it. If you can contribute more, do it.

Six-figure tick boxes (SFTB)

Imagine the year is 1986 and you and your best friend Charlie have just secured positions at a renowned retailer. Brimming with enthusiasm, you arrive early on your first morning, impeccably dressed in your company uniform, eager to conquer the world. Following some formal training and the issuing of name badges, you're summoned to the back office to meet with the company pension adviser. A tinge of apprehension fills the air as you both wonder what this meeting is all about.

Your family has always harboured a somewhat negative sentiment towards pensions, while Charlie's family has been more optimistic. The adviser presents a straightforward pension plan – you contribute 2 per cent of your wages and the company will match it with 10 per cent. Due to your preconceived notion that pensions are complicated and because you'd rather have a bigger pay cheque, a mindset inherited from your family, you politely decline. Charlie, viewing things from a different perspective, decides to join and confidently ticks the box on his form. That simple tick will pave the way for a six-figure future for Charlie in the 21st century – an embodiment of what financial advisers call 'six-figure tick boxes' (SFTBs).

SFTB decisions surface during my discussions with clients about pension contributions and stock market investment contributions. I consistently advocate for them to make sound financial decisions for their future selves, urging them to increase contributions frequently and aggressively. In meetings, I engage in a bit of mental gymnastics to help them grasp the concept of SFTBs: agree to a monthly increase, and you're paving the way for significant wealth in the future.

Most clients tend to underinvest, but when they achieve financial freedom down the road, they'll be grateful for these nudges. Encountering SFTBs is a regular occurrence with my clients, and I'm steadfast in ensuring the right choices are made with full comprehension of the implications.

Stay vigilant for SFTBs; they are lurking everywhere. These seemingly minor decisions can be the difference between a six-figure future and a missed opportunity.

Avoid default investment funds

Your employer's pension provider, or the provider's financial adviser, will choose a mixture of funds to make up your portfolio. That's fine, but if you want to grow wealth, it's better if you have some control over where your money is invested. I'll look at this more in Chapter 4.

The default fund with most pension schemes is not where you want long-term money to sit. Most investing is long term – even if you're going to leave the company and even if you're close to retiring. So, you ideally want to find a fund that is invested predominantly in global equities (the real wealth engine, and I explain these in Chapter 4).

When joining a company pension scheme, many individuals are often automatically invested into the default fund. These default funds typically invest in a mix of asset classes with the intention of suppressing volatility (which is the fluctuation of the fund values). However, it's worth highlighting that, as a result of this strategy, over extended periods it will likely produce lower returns than if you concentrated your assets in a higher-returning asset class, namely global equities.

Let's explain 'asset classes': global equities (shares),

bonds (corporate and government), property and commodities are all examples of asset classes. They're investments grouped together into a 'class' because they have similar characteristics.

'Allocation' means how your money is shared across the various asset classes. You could have 50 per cent in equities, and 25 per cent each in bonds and commodities, for example.

When you join the workplace pension scheme, the allocation is done for you. Opting instead for a fund exclusively focused on global equities, the world's premier wealth creation engine, can yield results that differ night and day over multiple decades. So, find out how you can choose which fund your contributions can be allocated to, remember SFTB, steer clear of the default fund and choose one focused on global equities.

Reject pension 'lifestyling' practices

Another SFTB involves the widespread practice of 'lifestyling' in pension plans leading up to retirement. This outdated strategy involves shifting investment from high-returning assets (global equities) to lower-return ones (fixed income and cash) before retirement. This practice was created at a time when people were forced to buy a pension annuity from their fund, so, ideally, they wanted to 'protect' the value in currency terms leading up to their retirement date.

Many people subjected to 'lifestyling' are unaware of its impact on their wealth. *A financial robot would turn lifestyling off.* I would also remove any option to lifestyle my own pension fund. Choosing whether to 'lifestyle' or not becomes another SFTB, so take action if necessary.

What happens if you don't opt to turn it off is that the pension scheme administrators will automatically switch your funds from high-returning assets to low-returning ones. In your head, exchange the word 'return with 'risk' – the scheme will refer to moving assets from 'high risk' to 'low risk'. But this is poor thinking about investing and is plain wrong.

To conclude, if you maximise your MMC (or contribute a bit more), invest the contributions predominately in a global equity fund and turn off lifestyling, you'll be well on the way to doing all you can on the pension front.

Financially optimal answers vs emotional answers

At various times in our lives we're presented with decisions to make. A good starting point when it comes to your financial decisions is to frame the 'What should I do?' question in two ways:

- £ What would a financial robot decide to do, as it's devoid of human emotions and answers everything in a supremely optimised way?
- £ What would a human do, filled as they are with human emotions and often making suboptimal decisions?

I feel that taking in these two extremes is a good starting point. For instance, in responding to a question such as 'How much cash should I keep on hand?', a financial robot would keep almost zero cash unless it was needed for a specific expense. But humans, on the other hand, usually keep way too much in cash, and from a financial point of view are happy to suffer suboptimal returns because they feel comfortable with the decision.

Another example is, 'Should we overpay our mortgage?' A financial robot would purely look at the mortgage rate vs the long-term expected return with investing and then decide accordingly. Whereas the human would tell themselves a story, maybe repeat a story from the past such as 'There's no better feeling than being mortgage free', and reach the answer emotionally rather than financially.

It's good to consider opposing views in life, the two extremes, because as humans we often steer towards the comfortable not the optimal. This is fine, as long as you know this.

Know when to deploy split decisions

Having worked with clients for close to 20 years, I've found that splitting decisions works really well for some situations. Of course, some decisions cannot be split – which job to take, whether to sell the house, what car to buy – but lots of decisions can, and when people split decisions they often feel a huge sense of relief.

They experience less remorse, the feeling that what they've decided was maybe not the best and they should have chosen the other option. So, let's look at a few examples of decisions that can be split. Your discretionary money is tight just now. Do you invest into an ISA or a pension?

This is a biggie. If the right or optimal answer is not clear, split the decision. If you have £500 to invest, invest £250 into each. Later on you can 'optimise' (choose to put the full £500 in one or the other) if the answer is clear.

Next up, do you overpay your mortgage or invest the additional money you have available instead? Again, if the answer is not clear then split the decision.

Another one is when you're unsure which fund to invest in if you've narrowed down your options to between two – well, you know the action: split the decision. Or, what if you're unsure how long to tie your cash up for, say, a fixed-term account – do you go for one year or two? Split the decision.

Having given lots of clients the encouragement to split decisions rather than do nothing, it's worked really well.

Another example is if you wanted to buy a new car and you were agonising about two purchasing options: either buy it for cash or take out a loan. Let's say the car costs £20k, so £20k cash or a loan of £20k over three years. In this situation, it's the perfect example for a split decision: use £10k cash and take out a £10k loan. The reason why split decisions work so well is because you have less remorse in the future if you feel either option was suboptimal.

Recognise when to stick

We make thousands of small decisions in our lives that ultimately result in big outcomes, but really there are perhaps only half a dozen key forks in the road during our lives. These are the big decisions: what university to go to, where to live, what career to pursue, who to marry, whether to have children, when to switch jobs.

A good general rule I share with clients is the concept of 'if the alternative is not overwhelmingly compelling, then the answer is to stick'. An example is: if you're offered a new job with only a minimal pay rise and you're also unsure about your new boss, this is not compelling enough to take it, so the answer is to stick.

You're thinking about relocating to a new city, but you're unsure about the traffic and you're on the fence about the healthcare there – not compelling enough, so stick. But what if you're offered a new job in a new city you've always wanted to live in?

And it's with a company you've always admired and your close friend who works there is very positive about the company and the role. This is compelling, so here you twist.

If it's overwhelmingly compelling, take action; if not, stick.

The FIRE community

Knowing your number, building up FU money and understanding your investing percentage are all concepts that have been brought together and supercharged to their ultimate conclusions by the 'financial independence, retire early' (FIRE) community.

Followers of this movement are serious, some might say militant, about creating their freedom from the shackles of the daily grind. They look to flex everything they can to achieve financial independence as early in life as they can.

It's a philosophy that has become more popular in recent years where people seek to maximise their savings percentage by increasing their income and aggressively decreasing their expenses through extreme frugality so that they can quickly accumulate the funds they will need to retire, ideally significantly earlier than the standard retirement age.

The benefits to this aggressive approach to saving can be seen here (where 1 represents your income and the decimal represents the percentage saved):

- £ At a savings rate of 10 per cent, it takes $(1-0.1)/0.1 = 9$ years of work to save for one year of living expenses.
- £ At a savings rate of 25 per cent, it takes $(1-0.25)/0.25 = 3$ years of work to save for one year of living expenses.
- £ At a savings rate of 50 per cent, it takes $(1-0.5)/0.5 = 1$ year of work to save for one year of living expenses.
- £ At a savings rate of 75 per cent, it takes $(1-0.75)/0.75 = 0.33$ years of work to save for one year of living expenses.

Achieving FIRE initially entails saving and investing a sum that is 25 times your average annual living expenses. Then what's known as the 4 per cent rule comes into play, and is based on two financial averages.

- £ First, it assumes that your investments will grow at an average rate of 7 per cent annually.
- £ Second, as the average rate of inflation is 3 per cent, you can safely withdraw 4 per cent of that growth every year, leaving 3 per cent behind to keep up with inflation.

If you're only spending the average growth from your investment portfolio, the theory is that you should never run out of money.

Depending on what stage you're at in your life and how much you have saved, you might be some way towards your 'annual expenditure × 25' figure already. Needless to say, you need to have cleared all your debt before embarking on this sort of a project, but it shows – perhaps in a way that's too extreme for some – just how in control we can be of our financial future if we pay close attention to our spending and savings percentages.

The FIRE community might not be abundantly rich on paper, or with plentiful supplies of cash to fall back on, but they're redefining what it means to be wealthy by focusing on freedom, independence and the liberty to live their lives just as they like. What could be richer than that?

Recognise and cut out poor financial habits

The first step to cutting out poor habits is to recognise what they are and when they occur. Here's a breakdown of some I have covered in this chapter and some that I will cover in the next one:

- £ spending a month's pay in two weeks and using payday loans and credit cards to make up the shortfall, which perpetuates a cycle of debt from which it's difficult to escape
- £ borrowing beyond your means and maxing out credit limits, without having any cash/assets behind you in case of emergency (perhaps losing your job)
- £ not protecting against poor health or death with the right insurance, which is dismissed as an unnecessary cost
- £ not maximising pension contributions from your employer's matching scheme because being paid more is preferable to you than building wealth with free money
- £ believing investing is 'risky' and not being willing to do any research to learn about it
- £ not taking advantage of all the benefits at work – eg private healthcare – again because this is seen as an unnecessary cost, whereas the benefits make a massive lifestyle difference
- £ spending windfalls and inheritances, wasting capital that comes in, rather than clearing debts and investing in appreciating assets
- £ not accounting for your tax bill if you are self-employed
- £ buying luxury items such as watches, holidays, gadgets, TVs and sound systems on finance – material

- £ items that will end up leaving a debt to service that you can't afford
- £ keeping up with the Joneses, regardless of income and common sense: the appearance of wealth (conspicuous consumption) occurs when people are sensitive about their standard of living in relation to their peers
- £ susceptibility to scams due to the lure of a quick win
- £ buying lottery tickets in the hope that all prayers will be answered
- £ elevating the importance of material items over experiences
- £ no drive for personal self-improvement, a sense of entitlement and a tendency to blame external factors for your financial fate
- £ not realising that the bulk of 'rich' people are self-made
- £ a reluctance to pay experts, always looking for a free or reduced-fee service
- £ not understanding and appreciating investment market volatility; it will happen, it should happen, we expect it.

As you're fighting against human behavioural traits that are often hard wired, this isn't an easy thing to do and requires persistence and hard work. You have picked up some tools in this chapter to set you on the right path and you will pick up some more when we dig into what investing is all about in the next one.

Enjoying this book?

I would love to hear from you.

Share what you have found useful, what has made you think differently or any questions that have come to mind.

Fill in the contact section on my website and I'd love to hear from you: **nobullmoney.co.uk**

Investing

Removing needless complication

Too many people seem to believe that financial advice is terribly complicated and mystifying, something that people outside the financial advice profession could never understand. This is wrong. In fact, financial advice is actually full of needless complication, not just created by people who work in the profession but sought out by those who don't.

We need to get to the facts and the fundamentals and keep things as simple as possible. Simplicity terrifies some financial advisers. It shouldn't, but it does. They go about elaborate ways of complicating what they do to justify what they charge their clients.

The focus of this chapter is to undo all that unnecessary complication and unravel these elaborate tapestries so that we're left with the simple, unadorned essentials. Investing, at its simplest, is the opportunity to benefit financially from the advance and growth of the great companies of the world. The global stock market captures the powerful force of human ingenuity.

In this chapter, I will set out my investing commandments, explain the jargon you might come across and help you understand the products, techniques and pitfalls, and how these tie in to the key principles and taking control.

When I address investing in this chapter, you'll see that I refer to 'the stock market'. The best way to think of the stock market is that it's a collection of real companies and real businesses selling real things (beer, computers, software) to real people – me and you.

Those who say they don't invest or don't engage with the stock market may not realise that, in some way, we are all connected to it. Whether directly or indirectly, it's a system that underpins much of modern life. We interact with stock market companies every time we buy a product or service. All of the products surrounding you are ultimately made by companies that are listed on the global stock markets.

People who might not want to invest in businesses on the stock market are happy to support these businesses by purchasing their products or paying for their services. A huge percentage of your life expenses will go towards supporting these big brands through your consumer choices.

You sleep in the stock market, drive the stock market, fly the stock market, eat the stock market, drink the stock market – hopefully you get the memo! The stock market is all around you; we're drowning in stock market companies.

The irony is that you're contributing to but not benefiting from the stock market's advance, which has been proven to be a great wealth creation engine over multiple decades. Being comfortable about investing in the stock market need not be scary.

The ten investing commandments

In my opinion, the points in the list below are the commandments to focus on in your investing journey. Why commandments? Because if you follow these, you'll see success. They're not 'suggestions' or 'nice to try' – they're actionable steps.

1. The stock market rewards the patient and punishes the rest.
2. Rising prices (inflation) can be your best friend or worst enemy.
3. Long-term returns come from investing in the great companies of the world (global equities).
4. All savings need to be automatic, or savings just won't happen.
5. Having and updating a financial plan is paramount. Having a portfolio is not a financial plan and outperformance is not a goal.
6. Disciplined behaviour will ensure your financial success.
7. The financial media do not have your financial future in mind.
8. There will always be negative news to report. Learn to ignore it.
9. Tax is likely to be your biggest expense, so learn to control its impact.
10. Never forget commandment one.

1. The stock market rewards the patient and punishes the rest

When it comes to how you approach investing, the main expression that will stand you in good stead is, 'The stock market rewards the patient and punishes the rest.' What does that mean? Essentially, no matter what the stock market does, don't make any rash decisions!

We've all heard of the fear of missing out, or FOMO. If you can fight this fear with regard to your investments, you'll be in a very strong place. JOMO is the joy of missing out. With investing you should avoid 'what's working now' and stick with 'what's always worked'.

Anything new, anything trending, anything exciting is 'what's working now'. Any good financial adviser will not have their head turned by the 'what's working now' fads of cryptocurrency, peer-to-peer lending, property bonds or anything else, so follow their lead.

All of these have made a big noise in recent years and been the hottest new tip on the block, but tips like these are usually temporary. Acting with equanimity through all fads and trends will ensure future financial success for you.

With JOMO, you do 'what's always worked', and that is investing in a collection of highly efficient, well-run, innovative global businesses with a proven history of delivering results, which ultimately means the capital value of your investment rises over multiple decades and rewards your patience.

Volatility: the natural ebbs and flows of the stock market

Stock markets are not going to rise in an unbroken trajectory from the day you start investing. There will be ups and downs along the way. Volatility is the friend of the long-term investor.

A key reason why investors receive increased returns is due to experiencing temporary volatility that is a necessary part of the investing process. It's a sign of your money maturity that you understand this and the benefits that volatility brings. Accepting volatility is a superpower for investors.

As a general rule, a global stock market portfolio is

rising approximately 75 per cent of the time and falling 25 per cent of the time (Decker 2023). Or, to put it another way, a dip is normal and to be expected. Accepting this and remembering it at times of turbulence is important.

A permanent loss comes only if you decide to sell out of your position. In layperson's terms, this means you'd permanently withdraw your investment in a particular asset – and I've already established that you're not going to be that kind of investor. Until then, it is only temporary volatility, and part of the ebb and flow of the stock markets. Remaining calm through deep temporary declines is the admission price to long-term wealth.

Once you move into the spending stage of your life and withdraw money from your investment portfolio (known in financial jargon as 'drawdown'), any market volatility may have more of an impact on your finances.

At this point, more than ever, the guidance of a financial adviser is important in helping you understand the challenges and inform your future decisions. I'll look at this more in Chapter 5.

Short-termism in lifetime investing

When it comes to investing, too many people have too short term a view. I've seen first hand just how worked up they get about short- and medium-term volatility in the stock market. To get concerned about this short-term volatility must mean they think they will need to spend or use all their capital in the short term. Otherwise, this market volatility is irrelevant. It's similar to the way people react when they see that house prices are slowing down. The prices declining should only be an issue for you if you need to sell your property today or very soon. Negative equity is an empty concept, one you don't need to worry about if you're not faced with the need to sell your house imminently. The reaction to market volatility is effectively the same thing.

If you are invested for the long term (as you should be) and there is no pressing need to use the capital during a downturn, then there is similarly no need to panic and/or potentially make a silly, knee-jerk decision.

Investing capital for the long term is about preserving the purchasing power of that money over your lifetime, not attacking the whole capital at any point, but strategically drawing down on this capital over the coming decades. Some investors have an inability to think of their capital working for them over 20, 30 or 40 years. Don't succumb to short-term thinking – life and investing are for the long term.

2. Rising prices (inflation) can be your best friend or worst enemy

Inflation is a silent killer to your wealth over time. It's the rising prices we all experience year after year. Think about how much a loaf of bread, a newspaper or a house cost 40 years ago – a lot less than they cost today. This is due to the decline of a currency's value over time. In a practical sense, it means that what you can buy with £1 in the future will be less than what you can buy with £1 today. So the name of the game is for your investments to outpace the force of inflation over the long term.

Here is a very simple example. In the 1980s, you could buy a 'mix-up' of sweets in a paper bag. The cheapest bag was 10 pence. That meant you would get ten one-penny sweets. In the 1990s, you'd get five or six sweets, as the larger ones now cost 2 pence. Now, a 10 pence mix-up is probably no longer available!

Inflation means that everyday goods and services that we all pay for in our ordinary lives become more expensive over time. As you can see from the example, the same amount of money means you can buy less as time goes on. It's worth noting also that the items are not necessarily more valuable or better quality, although that is the case sometimes.

So, you can see why investing is so important. Just leaving your money in cash means it earns little to no return once you factor in inflation. Inflation will eat away at its value, which over decades will have a serious impact.

If inflation was 3 per cent a year, within 24 years the *value* of the money you hold would enable you to buy only half of what you could today. To beat inflation, your money needs to work hard to stay ahead of it. And how can it do that? Your investments need to outpace the force of inflation over the long term. That means choosing assets that will potentially grow at a higher rate than inflation to increase your purchasing power (the value of your money) over time.

3. Long-term returns come from investing in the great companies of the world (equities)

In this book, I frequently refer to 'global equities', so it's important to understand exactly what I mean. Technically, global equities refers to money invested in companies through the purchase of shares, typically traded on stock exchanges. However, when I discuss global equity investing with my clients, I like to clarify it and focus on what we're really doing: investing in a collection of real businesses and companies that we interact with every day.

Instead of referring to 'the stock market', I prefer to call it 'the great companies of the world'. These are businesses that sell tangible products and services to real people, embodying human ingenuity. By investing in these companies, you're essentially betting on humanity's ability to innovate and create solutions that improve lives

– a belief that history has consistently supported. Global equities give you the opportunity to share in the financial success of this progress.

However, success requires discipline.

Owning global equities rewards those who can stay the course during their ownership. To fully embrace the potential of global equities, it's crucial to understand both their financial magic and their connection to human progress.

The harder you try, the worse you'll do
In no other endeavours in life is this statement true. When it comes to developing a skill, if you want to be world class at tennis, you need to practise and play; if you want to become a concert pianist, you have to practise and play.

To win and be world class at investing you need to practise perfect accuracy on day one by buying the right fund or fund mix, adding as much as you can to it as contributions are key – and then leaving it alone and never selling. You could select the right fund(s) with the help and advice of your financial adviser.

All the thinking is done on day one, then you should leave well alone apart from the action of buying more of the correct fund that you chose on day one. What will ensure that you become an investing loser is tinkering and listening to investment commentary.

Investing success is not only counterintuitive, it is also countercultural – two huge forces that are incredibly hard to fight against. The less you do, the better you'll do – it isn't easy to accept this, but it's true.

Do nothing and be lazy

Laziness is a skill that gets a pretty bad rap in all areas of life (poor old laziness). You can see why. To excel in most areas of human endeavour requires hard work, persistence, focus and energy. Without these you're unlikely to reach grade 8 in the piano or serve over 100 mph in tennis (109 mph is my personal best, thanks for asking!).

However, in investing, it can actually be your best friend. Forget about working away at something constantly, devoting all your energy to it and obsessing about it. The best way to reach financial success is to keep it simple and make fewer decisions.

Lazy, but patient, investors win. Hyperactive investors lose. A great motto, often attributed to renowned businessman and very successful investor Warren Buffett, states: 'Benign neglect, bordering on sloth, remains the hallmark of our investment process.'

This neglect and inactivity is all well and good as an idea, but in reality it can be difficult to achieve if you're brought up to believe that activity is the route to success in so many other areas of your life.

You may feel this especially acutely in times of market volatility or decline, but this is the time when you need to remain disciplined, sit tight and remember that your portfolio has been constructed for just this eventuality.

Looking too much at your portfolio, worrying and obsessing about it during a market decline, will fill you with pointless anxiety and keep tempting you to make a move that's not in your long-term financial interest. The less you look at it, the less needless anxiety you'll feel and ultimately the better you will do.

4. All savings and investments need to be automatic, or they just won't happen

One of the single most important practical pieces of behavioural guidance I can give you is to make your monthly investment savings automatic. If your savings are not automatic, they just won't happen.

I would also urge you to aggressively nudge up your automatic monthly savings to a level you can (just about) afford. Once you move into your spending stage of life, the biggest missed opportunity would be not having continued to nudge up your monthly contributions over time. It could make a very serious difference to your spending years.

In round numbers, let's say you're contributing £500 per month currently, and £1,000 is easily achievable, make the change to nudge up the automatic payments and get the return on that money over the long run.

Invest monthly and the amount should feel slightly uncomfortable

This is part of the key principle to pay yourself first. You can never invest too much. As I mentioned in Chapter 3, when clients ask me how much they should be investing and when they should start, my answer is always the same: more and yesterday. Setting up automatic monthly payments to an investment account is the most effective route to your future financial success.

5. Having and updating a financial plan is paramount

Just having an investment portfolio is not a financial plan and outperformance in isolation of a financial plan is not a goal. As I discussed in Chapter 3, you must create and regularly maintain a financial plan. Have a look at that section again to remind yourself what a good financial plan should contain.

You should only make a change to or tweak an investment portfolio if your financial plan has fundamentally changed, not the other way around. Do not switch out of an investment portfolio as a consequence of how the markets are behaving, because your portfolio should have been set up with the foresight of knowing that there will be fluctuation. This is baked into your financial plan. If your financial plan has changed, then your portfolio may be changed.

You need to keep working on your financial plan and leave the investment portfolio to do its job. Ultimately, the investment portfolio funds your financial plans and all the transitions that your life throws at you.

Schedule in an annual review of your financial plan

It's time we all grew up a bit. As a society, as individuals, as investors. I don't mean growing up chronologically; I'm talking about acting like a mature adult when it comes to addressing money.

Life expectancy is increasing across the globe; we're living longer and longer and the effect of this seems to be that many of us think we can have an extended adolescence. We can carry on being carefree well into our twenties, thirties or forties – maybe postponing adult decisions forever. The irony is that, with an ageing population and greater and greater strain being placed on state pension funds around the world, the sooner we get our financial act together in life the better.

It's vital to start planning now, both to smooth financial highs and lows during your working years and to prepare for a retirement that seems to be getting further and further away every year – the gap between when you might want to stop working and when you might live until just keeps getting bigger.

You need to take responsibility, take control of your financial affairs and take advice. It might be painful in the short term, and you might hear advice you don't like, but it's for your own good. The sensible response to considered and constructive criticism or advice is to take it on board and act on it, not put your fingers in your ears or mute the truth-teller because they make you feel a bit uncomfortable.

6. Disciplined behaviour will ensure your financial success

When I first started out as a financial adviser, I saw myself doing what every other adviser did: managing money. Then one day, it dawned on me that all the issues I dealt with day in, day out were created by the people, not the money. I realised that managing the humans was more fundamental to success than managing their assets – a lot more!

Humans aren't rational, and, as I pointed out in Chapter 1, sometimes they inherit deeply unhelpful attitudes to money. We all come from a standing start and need to learn, adapt and evolve as part of our journey through life. Often, in planning our lifetime finances, we need to modify how we think and operate by being shown when we're making mistakes so we can be nudged and encouraged towards the right decisions.

My experience with hundreds of clients has shown me that my role is much more about behaviour modification than money management. I only spend a fraction of my time with a client addressing the financial issues; the majority I devote to behavioural coaching to cut out the mistakes.

With a topic as fundamentally important to your life success as this, you will notice I refer to behaviour throughout this book, and it runs clearly through all the advice I've given so far, but to truly take it on board we need to go under the bonnet so you can understand just how deeply it drives you (in ways you don't even notice) and how closely intertwined it is with your future financial wellbeing.

The birth of behavioural finance

It's America in the 1970s. The US economic picture is dominated by inflation, unemployment, high oil prices and recession. Meanwhile, a small group of economists and social scientists are questioning the idea that humans always make rational and predictable decisions when it comes to money.

Two of the leading proponents, Daniel Kahneman and Amos Tversky, are psychologists rather than economists. While at the time, this seemed like a crazy challenge to established economic thinking, it makes sense that they had a background in exploring the human psyche.

All economic theories assume that humans aren't affected by their emotions when making financial choices and just do the rational thing when they have a decision to make. But this handful of academics kept working away at this new idea.

They became increasingly convinced that traditional theories don't tell the full story. If we really want to understand how people make financial decisions, they say, we also need to consider more carefully how emotional and irrational humans can be.

Between them, these academics became the founding fathers of behavioural economics and behavioural finance. This was the very beginning of the community that I, my fellow behavioural financial advisers and coaches, and growing numbers of investors are now a part of.

It was a revolutionary idea at the time that, unsurprisingly, didn't take off immediately. However, this community started to grow and grow, while behavioural thinking was working its way into many other sectors too, such as politics, business and retail.

The story of Kahneman, Tversky and their peers is well known and referenced by multiple universities in their economics programmes. A brief summary can also be found on the NASDAQ website (see References for full details).

When one of the founding academics, Richard Thaler, won the Nobel Prize for Economics in 2017, that confirmed its acceptance as one of the most important and defining ideas of our era. From an idea born in recession-hit America of the 1970s, behavioural finance has created a community of adherents that makes our profession proud.

The behavioural finance community continues to expand and develop today. I see it in my own experience among fellow financial advisers. There was a time when it was just a small huddle of us nurturing this new philosophy in our profession, but there are more and more of us every time I look.

It may have started as a niche viewpoint, but that niche is growing daily, monthly, yearly. Independent financial advisers are on the front line and deal with humans every day, so it shouldn't be a surprise that they should be the early adopters, but there are big asset managers only just cottoning on to the insights of behavioural thinking and employing them at a more corporate level.

One of the things I like most about the behavioural finance community, and the behavioural discipline in general, is the mix of people we attract from a variety of different backgrounds. It's relevant to so many fields. Obviously financial advice and behavioural science, but also areas as varied as management consultancy, think tanks, the media, risk profiling and fintech (financial technology). This is why I believe behavioural finance advice is so powerful: because it channels the insights of so many areas and is open to input from such a broad spectrum of disciplines. It allows us to keep developing ever more sophisticated methods so we can give our clients the best insights and service possible.

As with any new discipline in any profession, there are some dissenting voices. Many advisers still think they manage money, not people. I don't share their point of view, of course, but I respect their opinions. A lot of their resistance shows a misunderstanding of what we're trying to do. We're not here to replace the traditional and technical side of financial advice where these detractors would claim the 'real value' is.

There's a place at the table for everyone. Behavioural finance is not a threat to traditional thinking. It's here to complement that, to make what we've already got even better. It's to contribute to the body of knowledge we've amassed and to enhance the cause and profile of our profession. It is the element of financial planning that can't be commoditised.

Benefits of the behavioural approach
Hopefully you can now see the benefits of using the behavioural finance approach to your investing, wealth building and future planning. Here are a couple of other reasons why I recommend this method over any other.

- £ **Cuts out financial mistakes**: The fundamental purpose of mature financial behaviour is to cut out as many naïve financial mistakes as possible. If you acknowledge you are susceptible to these mistakes, you can tackle them head on. You can take the emotion out of financial planning and stop natural human biases from derailing your carefully laid financial plans. I will discuss common mistakes later in this chapter. Behavioural awareness stops you from exiting the market at the first sign of a downturn, when it may actually be better to sit tight, or overestimating your abilities when it comes to managing your money, or thinking that trying to time the markets is a good idea.

£ **Answers the expensive questions:** The expensive questions are the ones that will have the big, life-changing answers: 'Am I going to be OK?' 'If I don't wake up tomorrow morning, is my family going to be provided for?' 'When can I retire?' These are the things that keep us awake in the early hours. Taking the actions I have recommended in Chapters 2 and 3 will set you on the right path, and you can then work with a financial adviser to obtain expertise and insight into investment and help you reduce behavioural bias.

Challenges to applying the behavioural approach
It's human nature to be foolish when it comes to money and investing, and most people are full of biases when they're about to make an important financial decision. The problem is that biases stop us making the right decision for our financial wellbeing or the optimal choice for our future happiness.

Biases tell us to invest in cryptocurrencies because that's what everyone else is doing (known as bandwagon bias). They convince us we can make better financial decisions in our lives than impartial financial professionals (over-confidence bias). And they keep unpleasant memories front and foremost when we make a financial decision (negativity bias). The list of biases goes on, but you get my point. It's impossible to stop humans being human, so we have to adapt to this.

Below is a list of the most common biases and how they apply to your financial decision making. I'm sure you can probably spot elements of your own behaviour in many of them, and now you can use behavioural awareness to overcome the ones you are susceptible to.

- **£ Anchoring**: This is when there's a tendency to rely too much on the first piece of information we receive when we're making a decision. When we do this, we might overlook or ignore information that could be more helpful to us in the process.
- **£ Availability heuristic**: This is when we overestimate the likelihood of an event happening. This is based on how recently we think it last happened or because we have a strong recollection of what it was like at the time. The best example of this is a financial crisis such as a recession, but these are actually relatively rare.
- **£ Bandwagon effect**: We believe something to be true, or do something that seems sensible because others do. Other terms for this include herd mentality and groupthink. Just because other people are doing the same thing as you doesn't mean it's right, especially when it comes to financial decisions.
- **£ Buyer's remorse**: This is when you feel regret after making a purchase. This often happens when you've made a large investment or deciding to make the investment was difficult. A good example of this is buying property abroad.
- **£ Confirmation bias**: Looking for information that agrees with our beliefs or preconceptions. This could result in finding a financial adviser who'll tell you what

you want to hear, rather than solid advice that's helpful.
- **Conjunction fallacy**: Making incorrect assumptions, such as 'I'll lose money if I invest', despite the fact that returns are usually positive.
- **Declinism**: When you think things were better in the past, especially in comparison to where you think things are going in the future. This prevents people from making changes for the better and they stick to what they've always done instead.
- **Decision fatigue**: When you've made a lot of decisions in a short space of time, and you find yourself making wrong or questionable decisions. Making too many choices at once means you won't get the outcomes you want. This can also lead to 'decision avoidance', where we choose not to make any decisions because there are too many options to choose from.
- **Ego depletion**: When we make bad decisions after making several good ones because we believe there's only so much willpower we can call upon. For example, a smoker trying to quit having a 'reward' of a cigarette after two weeks of not smoking.
- **Empathy gap**: Not understanding how much feelings or emotions play into our decision-making process. Emotion is particularly powerful here.
- **Endowment effect**: Wanting more to give something up than you would be prepared to pay to get it in the first place. For example, people expect buyers to give them a lot of money for their car or home. Why? It seems more valuable because *they* own it.
- **Exaggerated expectation**: When we imagine the worst, but the evidence turns out to be better than we thought. For instance, you might feel disappointed when your investment portfolio returns a lower result

than the previous year, even though it's still given a good return.

- **£ Fundamental attribution error**: This exhibits itself as a tendency to blame others when things go wrong instead of being objective. You made a bad investment and blame the person who suggested it, rather than accepting responsibility yourself.
- **£ Gambler's fallacy**: Thinking that what may or may not happen in the future depends on the past, when it doesn't. The best example of this is people assuming that a coin that's landed the same way several times in a row will do the opposite on the next flip.
- **£ IKEA effect**: People put a disproportionately high value on something they've assembled themselves (eg flatpack furniture) regardless of the quality of the end result. For example, in a period when equity markets have performed well, anyone who's done a bit of research and picked some funds will overestimate their skill when these funds subsequently provide decent returns (in isolation).
- **£ Loss aversion**: The pain we feel when we have losses outweighs the joy we feel after equivalent gains at a rate of 2:1. Imagine losing £50,000 compared to gaining £50,000, following a £100,000 investment. The money has moved by the same amount, yet the loss has a far greater impact on our emotions.
- **£ Money illusion**: Focusing on the face value of money rather than its purchasing power (where the real value is). The bigger the numbers, the more we feel it. For instance, we know that £20 won't buy as much in the future as it does today, yet we struggle to equate this to larger sums. Convert this to £200,000 – the impact of inflation is still relative, yet we fail to pay it the same credence.

- £ **Negativity bias**: As humans, we're much better at remembering bad memories compared to good ones. This tendency affects our future decision making. Why? Because we use examples of past bad experiences as evidence that the same will happen again.
- £ **Normality bias**: When someone refuses to plan for something they've never experienced. None of us has experienced retirement before we get to it, but it's good to plan for it all the same.
- £ **Omission bias**: When we think harmful actions are worse than equally harmful inactions.
- £ **Optimism bias**: Assuming that making a decision will lead to a positive outcome; for example, millions of people play the lottery and think they have a good chance of winning (but don't put money into their savings).
- £ **Overconfidence bias**: Being too confident in your own ability to do something. That's why people will go with their own decisions rather than listening to a professional (who's impartial to the outcome).
- £ **Paralysis by analysis**: Failing to make a decision due to overthinking a situation. We 'paralyse' our decision-making ability, which can happen when there are too many options.
- £ **Post-purchase rationalisation**: Trying to convince yourself that a recent purchase was a good idea and good value. It can involve making 'rational arguments' to support this.
- £ **Projection bias**: An assumption that your future self will share your current views and values. This can mean that you work towards a goal that was important when you first set it, but isn't any longer.
- £ **Regret aversion**: Avoiding making decisions because of a fear or regret.

- **£ Restraint bias**: Being unable to show restraint when tempted, such as thinking you're in control of your spending and credit card debts.
- **£ Risk compensation**: Increasing risks when we assume safety increases alongside it. In investing, this might mean when someone knows they have a guaranteed income for retirement so take more of a risk with the pension pot. They then may be severely disappointed when the fund declines.
- **£ Status quo bias**: Being happier if things can stay the same, even if there are potentially better options.
- **£ Sunk cost fallacy**: Justifying increased belief in a decision based on previous ones, despite new evidence suggesting the decision was probably wrong. The more you invest, the harder it becomes to let go.

7. The financial media do not have your financial future in mind

Being disciplined means never reacting to the ebbs and flows of the stock markets – in essence selling at the wrong time because you're scared – however tempting it may be and whatever the financial media is screaming at you.

This is where managing your behaviour and emotions is everything. If you work with a financial adviser (see Chapter 5), they will have constructed your financial plan and portfolio to accommodate the natural ups and downs of the global markets over the long term.

Success with investing is 'time in the markets' and never trying to 'time the markets' (these are discussed later in this chapter). Most market commentators need to generate revenue, and they don't have your family's financial future in mind when they write clickbait articles just to sell advertising space.

Redefining the news (negative events world service)
The news is something to be very wary of. It always follows the same sort of pattern: you switch on the TV to see a production line of reports of political turmoil across the globe and you're told that the markets are plummeting in response.

Or you pick up a paper to read that a country in the West and a country in the East are about to go to war, with the global economy on the brink of an unprecedented meltdown. Your smartphone continues to bleep and ping all day with fresh updates on the end of the world and what it means (nearly always bad) for your finances, and you don't know what to do about it all.

In reality, this conveyor belt of doom and negativity will never end. Sometimes it seems to exist separately from what is happening in the markets, and certainly at quite some distance from what it means for you and your investment portfolio and financial plan. If you are smart, you will realise that the news is forever screaming about a new catastrophe and telling investors what to do, but by the next day will have moved on to something else entirely.

It veers wildly from financial 'crisis' to financial 'panic' and, if it needed saying, this is primarily to get your attention and not provide you with measured, sensible advice. The media are all about today, immediacy, what's happening right now and why it matters right now. They have absolutely no interest in anything other than the short term.

For the news media, long term is about wondering whether the story they're breaking in the morning has got the legs to make it all the way to the evening news bulletin at 6 pm. So, their take on the news and what's happening in the markets and across the global economy is wildly at odds with the long-term stance a sensible investor will be taking towards their investments, which will have a time horizon of decades, not hours, into the future.

I can't state this starkly or often enough: the media are not interested in your financial wellbeing. They are focused on selling papers or attracting viewers or clicks so they can sell advertising space.

A business news bulletin that opens with the line 'The markets have dipped by -3 per cent today but this holds no threat to sensible investors with a well-diversified portfolio geared for the long term' is something that you are never going to see happening. Why? Because, as the old media adage goes, if you're not panicking, they're not doing their job.

Social media has made the problem even worse, so there's now no escape from the constant drip feed of calamity. Sensation, pessimism and negativity sell. Facts, optimism and positivity do not.

I can make light of it, but the problem is that it does influence investor behaviour, and encourages them to behave irrationally in the form of making knee-jerk reactions or extreme, and extremely inappropriate, responses.

Financial success demands healthy financial behaviour, but most of what the media does is to stoke and encourage misbehaviour. It appeals to base, destructive human instincts such as fear and greed, and no good can come from this, so shutting out this negativity is important and vital to behaving your way to wealth.

One way to think of what the media serve up is as a sort of financial pornography. And if you look back over the years you can see that this is something that is absolutely nothing new or by any means restricted to our generation.

Think back at some of the headlines you've seen about stock market crashes, people losing money, global organisations suddenly disappearing. You'll start to realise how the media have been trying to terrorise us with new reasons not to invest for years and years and years. Meanwhile, the stock market has continued its steady advance.

If you or one of your ancestors had been persuaded away from investing by any of these media scare stories of years gone by, you, or they, would have missed out on the returns that followed. That's a fact.

8. There will always be negative news to report, so learn to ignore it

What bearing will today's crisis have on your 30-year retirement plan? Let's be honest, the majority of modern investors aren't still reeling from the decline in the early 2000s.

Look at the devastating impact of Black Monday almost 40 years ago. It was catastrophic at the time for investors, but they, and the market, recovered. It's natural to panic when you see those huge headlines everywhere, but please, please don't. You'll be fine!

9. Tax is likely to be your biggest expense – learn to control its impact

For most people, tax is likely the single biggest expense they'll face in their lifetime – bigger than their mortgage, childcare or even their weekly Waitrose habit. But because it's usually deducted quietly from your payslip each month, you rarely *see* the full number. Out of sight, out of mind. That's a problem, because if you don't acknowledge tax as the major cost, you won't take steps to manage it. Learning how to legally and intelligently control your tax bill is one of the most powerful tools in achieving financial freedom. Ignore it and you're leaving serious money on the table.

Two behavioural traits of the ideal investor

I'm sure I could come up with a long list of bullet points for you on what makes the ideal investor, but the two most important ones are humility and teachability.

Let's start with humility. This is you understanding that when it comes to financial planning, you can't do it alone. Actually, you can do it alone if you like but it's unlikely you'll succeed. Year after year, study after study shows that the DIY investor achieves lower returns.

For instance, the annual Quantitative Analysis of Investor Behavior (QAIB) report from DALBAR (Data Analysis for Leaders in Business), an independent research firm specialising in the financial services industry, has data on how investors fare on their own compared to the professionals (and those who use an adviser). Furthermore, the online trading site Capital.com tracks the portfolios of its users and reports that more than 70 per cent of DIY investors lose money (see References).

I'll tell you a short story to show you what I mean. The story is a made-up example but the sort of evidence it's based on is similar to those often told in the financial advice profession.

Let's say 100 people are asked to take part in an investment challenge. The group is split into two. Fifty people have access to all the latest analysis and news, and let's also say they can trade their investments with zero commission and fees. The other 50 people are not allowed to trade and simply have to hold the general stock market, such as a global equity fund.

What studies repeatedly show is that the non-active group who are not allowed to trade and must simply sit on their hands would on average wipe the floor with the investors who are free to trade as they like.

The traders will fall into all sorts of traps informed by bad decisions and, in short, their tinkering and misinformed activity means they will end up underperforming their own investments because they will be buying and selling at the wrong times and reacting and responding in the wrong way. Their actions, aimed at increasing their investment, would be more damaging than doing absolutely nothing. If that's not a humbling thought, I don't know what is.

Teachability and a willingness to learn should naturally follow from the humility in realising that our own uninformed efforts could do more harm than good when it comes to investing. Teachability is different from intelligence. It's not a question of whether the investor will understand complex investment analysis (they don't necessarily need to), it's more about their mindset and goes hand in hand with humility. It's about being open minded enough to seek advice when they know they have exceeded the boundaries of their knowledge, to learn from this and to act on it in future.

Understanding risk

Risk is one of those words that is frequently bandied about but is meaningless without context. Investors will often say they want to avoid all risks with their investments, but this is not possible. Saying you don't want any risk with your investment is like saying you don't want any oxygen with your air. What an inexperienced investor often means when they say they don't want any risk is that they don't want any volatility, but the mature investor understands that risk is an essential part of investing and volatility is inevitable over the long term.

It's helpful to give some context by separating risk into

informed risk and uninformed risk. These can be seen in Figure 2, with each scale containing the same ten individual financial options. Moving your thinking from uninformed risk to informed risk is a key transition in achieving money maturity.

Within informed risk, we can break this down further into three different flavours of risk: volatility, inflation and permanent loss of capital. When making investment and financial decisions, it helps to be aware of and clear about what is at risk of happening in each of these instances, rather than thinking of risk as just an abstract threat, unconnected to the ultimate eventualities.

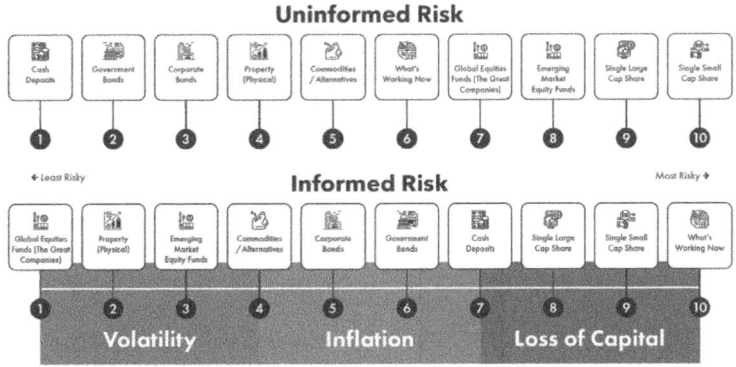

Figure 2: Uninformed vs informed risk

- **£ Volatility:** If we take history as our guide (and it is the only guide we have), a globally well-diversified equity portfolio (a well-spread collection of the great businesses of the world) has outpaced inflation comfortably over multiple decades. Any permanent loss while invested in a globally well-diversified equity portfolio will be as a result of a human decision to sell at the wrong time. Volatility, and remaining calm when it happens, is the entry price to long-term wealth. Being calm through all market declines is the preserve of those with healthy investment behaviour. Don't be distracted by the temporary stock market declines; expected volatility or the unpredictability of the investment markets over the short term.

- £ **Inflation:** This is the silent wealth destroyer – the slow but steady and sure increase in prices over decades that can outpace your investments if you don't take it into account. If inflation is increasing more than your total return, then every year you 'invest' you are losing value and slowly losing money. Money is not currency; it's purchasing power. What will your money be able to buy in the future? Will it be able to buy the same number of beers/burgers/cars that it can today?

- £ **Permanent loss of capital:** This is the most dangerous flavour of risk. Examples of this would be investing in a business that ends up collapsing, fraud or criminal activity, or investing in a single company that goes bust. The outcome from uninformed risk = low investment returns. Frankly, most people are invested in the wrong long-term asset mix, ie not enough in global equities and too much in global bonds (both government and corporate) and other alternative asset classes (examples being private equity, hedge funds, real estate, infrastructure, commodities, forestry, etc), so, over the long term, their portfolio will achieve lower returns. Low returns are, however, not clear to see: they're the returns you didn't get – the money you didn't build up, the holidays you didn't go on, the money you could have spent on your grandkids. A well-constructed portfolio tilted towards the high-returning asset class will counteract the silent, tasteless risk of low returns.

Framing risk correctly is vital in making optimal decisions for your financial future. It is a necessary part of the investing process and something you need to constantly revisit if you're to avoid big mistakes. You'll be dancing with risk whether you like it or not; you just need to choose which type of risk you're prepared to dance with.

As I mentioned earlier when I touched on investing, everyone has a different level of risk tolerance. Remember this when you're in a couple. There are tests you can do to see what yours is, and it will show you how much money you're comfortable investing (as a proportion of what you have available) as well as how much volatility in your funds you can accept. I've put a link to Merrill Lynch's version in the References.

Common investor mistakes

None of us sets out to make mistakes, but when it comes to finance it can be easy for the uninitiated to stray from the optimal path, even with the best of intentions. I'm far from perfect, but I continue to develop my knowledge and learn from my mistakes and, more importantly, the mistakes of others.

As they say, an expert is someone who's made all the mistakes. Fortunately, I'm in a business that has fast learning built into it: as a financial adviser, I'm exposed to many stories and mistakes, positive and negative, which result in learning more and put me on the path to achieving wisdom.

Here are some real-life financial mistakes that we can all fall into the trap of making. It's not an exhaustive list, but they help to illustrate the sort of things you should be trying to avoid and the bad behaviour that can undermine your best-laid financial plans.

1. **Overcomplicating matters:** There are usually simple solutions to most problems. Don't think complex means good or better; it invariably doesn't. Naïve complexity is everywhere in investing. As I stated at the beginning of this chapter, I am a strong advocate for simplicity.
2. **Over-precision:** This is a closely related problem, which is when we worry too much about the specific details rather than getting on with taking good-enough action with finances. Don't let perfect be the enemy of good.
3. **Overcomplicating for profit:** As an insider of the financial advice industry, it boils my blood what some firms charge for something that can be achieved for sometimes a tenth of the price. I see large 'investment advisers' charging clients 1.5–3 per cent for a basic investment portfolio, when the same can be achieved for something closer to 0.2 per cent – and the kicker is the returns from the lower-charging portfolio will likely be superior over the long term.

The wealth that is extracted from novice investors is immoral, bordering on white-collar crime, in my opinion. These investment advisers look to overcomplicate for profit, baffle clients, impress them with slick brochures and add an allure of complexity to justify their fees and existence.

It's frustrating that people fall for these marketing tricks time and time again, but when you're uncertain about what to do with your money and where to put it, these managers seem compelling.

I'm hoping that this book will guide you away

from them and towards a reputable financial adviser. Do your due diligence before you part with your money.
4. **Confusing information with wisdom**: To paraphrase American businessman and investor Charlie Munger's 1994 speech to the USC Business School, 'Wisdom doesn't come across well in a classroom.' He's right. We're certainly not lacking in information in the world at the moment, but this is useless without wisdom in choosing, applying and actioning it. Take your knowledge and leverage it to make better decisions.
5. **Impatience**: Believing wealth is a 'get rich quick' game is an error. Creating wealth is a 'get rich slow' scheme, despite the stories the financial media will bombard you with. Shortcuts don't work. Don't try them.
6. **Constant monitoring**: We live in a world of instant information, and most of the time expect instant answers. When it comes to investing, this might mean checking your investment accounts every day. With the proliferation of online investment platforms, checking 24 hours a day is now possible. This behaviour is not good for your long-term financial wellness. The less you look, the better you'll feel, act and ultimately behave. It is total madness and only leads to knee-jerk decisions, underperformance and feeling financially anxious. You don't check the price of your house daily, so don't constantly check your investment accounts. Think of investing like a bar of soap: the less you touch it, the more you'll have!

At the end of the day, the more investment units you continue to acquire, the more wealth you'll build long term. Checking the price of these units daily when you could be holding them for at least 30 years is unhealthy behaviour. It's as useful as planting potatoes and then ripping them out of the ground to check the roots are still there. They are – leave them alone. Instead of checking your investment values, research something new, acquire new knowledge. Learn a language, pick up a musical instrument, join a book club. Or just go out for a walk with the dog!

7. **'Get rich quick' scams:** You've probably heard occasional news stories about unsuspecting investors who got scammed by some ruthless opportunists who took their money by dangling the promise of unbelievably bountiful returns in record time frames. There are generally two types of unfortunate investor who fall for this type of ruse, one of whom I have genuine sympathy for; the other, not so much. One falls for the scam through deception; the other finds themselves there out of greed. The stories of innocent elderly people who have been callously conned into parting with their life savings make everybody's blood boil. It's wrong, criminally and morally, and there can be little defence for those who make their living this way.

The other type of victim needs to take more of the blame for their own actions. They allowed their personal greed to silence every last doubting voice in their head before handing the money over, and will be able to reflect on their error at leisure. Savvy investors know that the most certain way to get rich is to do so slowly and not by chasing after propositions that seem too good to be true. Behaving yourself with wealth means relying on the methods that have always worked, not giving in to behaviour and instincts that suggest a shortcut. And those are methods from professional financial advisers, not your relatives (remember the taxi driver's grandad?). The only place that shortcuts get you to quickly is poverty.

8. **Thinking financial success is down to intelligence and not behaviour:** The greatest tests you will face as a long-term investor will be emotional ones. All the information and intelligence in the world cannot protect you from how you are going to feel when you're experiencing the ups and downs of the emotional investing cycle. How you choose to behave at these times is fundamental to your long-term financial success. You'll be a successful long-term investor if you invest in what's always worked, which is a well-diversified collection of large companies that can be accessed via a global equity investment fund.

9. **Ignoring your future self**: Failing to understand the concept of 'your future self' is a common mistake. Most people don't face immediate financial problems – they manage their day-to-day needs. However, this false sense of security often leads to neglecting long-term planning, which sets the stage for future financial difficulties. Many struggle to connect with their future selves, seeing them as entirely separate people, which makes planning ahead feel less urgent. True financial maturity comes when you realise that financial planning is for the benefit of your future self. While it can be challenging to think ten, 20 or even 50 years ahead, the sooner you embrace this mindset, the more your future self will thank you.

10. **Thinking of your investments as 'funds' rather than asset classes:** I try to explain to my clients that we're doing 'asset class investing' and we use 'investment funds' to access these asset classes. An

investment fund is where your money (investment) joins with the money of other investors into one pot, so all investors will experience the returns of that fund. The returns for each investor will all be slightly different as they bought and sold into it at different times. Very high-level asset classes are split between equities (owning a small percentage of a company listed on the stock market) and then fixed income (also referred to as bonds), which is basically lending your money to governments and companies.

Fixed-income assets (bonds) are generally considered less volatile and also produce lower long-term returns, particularly when you factor in inflation. Most portfolios are split between equities and bonds, and equities are split between developed markets (those which have been around for hundreds of years) and emerging markets (which have been around for a shorter time and are less developed).

Within that, there are small and large companies, as well as value companies (those considered undervalued relative to their accounting fundamentals, often offering steady dividends and investment returns) and growth companies (those expected to grow at an above-average rate, often reinvesting profits into expansion rather than paying dividends) – think your typical big tech company.

The split between equities and bonds is what will drive the bulk of your returns. Inexperienced investors focus too much on the funds themselves or even the fund managers, and not enough on the overall asset allocation. The asset allocation is more of a driver for investment returns than the actual fund or fund manager you choose.

In my years as a financial adviser, I've had the opportunity to watch how humans react during a stock market downturn (framed as a temporary decline). It's important for you to understand that the market doesn't make mistakes. It does what it's always done, which is move in cycles. Once the decline is over, it will continue its advance.

When the market's rising, everything is fine and I tend not to hear from clients too much, but when the market takes a turn – as it naturally will – certain identifiable patterns emerge. As the market moves in its cycles, the investors themselves are also moving in their own cycles.

In its rawest form, the investor cycle moves from greed to fear, then fear to greed. During a market decline, fear is what the investor is feeling. When the market is flying and advancing, greed kicks in. They may not recognise it or admit it, but this is almost certainly the case.

Dealing with a market decline

A market decline is a test for the amateur. The amateur wants to react, thinking it will help the situation. The expert, on the other hand, knows that doing nothing will get them through it. It's fair to say that financial advisers actually earn their money during a decline.

It's the point where advisers step forward, hold out their hand and act as caring listeners to their clients, guiding them and keeping them on course. Advisers remove anxiety and help their clients understand that everything that's going on is normal and expected, and it too will pass.

Clients find it very hard to experience and go through a market decline, particularly a deep one. That anxiety can be heightened if the market decline begins soon after the start of a new client–adviser relationship.

However, this is also where the behavioural adviser's three-pronged approach comes into its own. First, you've built their financial life plan. Second, you've funded it with investment contributions. Third, you are equipped to coach them through these wobbles because you understand their biases and emotions. The plan and the portfolio are pointless without the crucial behavioural coaching.

As an adviser, I have 'skin in the game'. I am invested in the same portfolios as my clients. I am invested in my 100 per cent global equities portfolio – so when my clients feel fearful in relation to their portfolio, its return and its value, I feel the same. I will also feel the full force of any stock market volatility.

The wrong way to think about market declines

The surest path to making poor investment decisions is to focus on short-term market movements. What we lose sight of during times of uncertainty is that the value of our portfolio (or that of an index quoted in the newspaper) on any particular day is no reflection of our progress towards financial independence. Obsessing about this number is the first step on the road to worrying about countless factors outside of your control. This is not a recipe for investment success.

Below are the most common mistakes I see investors make about market declines.

Not knowing the numbers going in

As I mentioned in the first of the ten investment commandments at the beginning of this chapter, it's important to understand and remember that the global stock market generally declines about 25 per cent of the time and increases in value around 75 per cent of the time. These are great odds: 3 to 1 in your favour.

Not sticking to the plan

Your financial plan is the important thing to focus on, not the temporary declines, volatility or unpredictability of investment markets.

Blaming the adviser

You may be more aware of volatility in the markets if you've just started to work with a financial adviser, but it's not a reflection on their skill or quality if your portfolio has declined soon after they've taken over its management.

The market, not the adviser, will dictate the returns. The market has far more influence on your portfolio than the adviser, who is giving you access to the market. If you decide to switch financial adviser because the market has declined, during the next temporary decline, which is probably just around the corner, you may switch again.

You could be constantly changing advisers, when the issue is you and not them. Don't switch advisers when you need to switch your investor behaviour – meaning what you're doing. Realise that a professional adviser is there to help and shouldn't be the focus of any perceived underperformance.

Succumbing to the money illusion

Let's say you invest £100,000 with adviser A, and during the time you're investing with them the markets have been favourable, making the portfolio worth £150,000. You then decide to work with adviser B, who takes over the management of the £150,000 portfolio, where the chosen asset classes are more or less the same. You then experience 'money illusion' – anchoring the value of what you think you've invested as £150,000 now rather than the original £100,000.

A market decline happens very soon after starting work with adviser B and your portfolio goes down to £135,000.

You wrongly think you invested £150,000, which has now reduced to £135,000.

This is technically correct, but an unwise statement to make. You invested £100,000 in the markets, so the portfolio now is still higher than when you originally invested; however, as you switched adviser you have 'anchored' the amount you originally invested (£100,000) to the amount when you switched the portfolio (£150,000). There may have been a small tweak to the fund by adviser B, but it's still broadly invested in the same asset classes.

Making statements instead of asking questions

This is common when an investor is unfamiliar with a particular investment they hold. I don't make statements to my plumber or my doctor. I ask questions, because I don't know the subject area well enough. Yet, in investing and finance, people make statements such as 'I should never have invested'. Instead, they should ask the question, 'Should I be worried about what's happening now?'

Don't say, 'We need to change the fund.' A sensible question instead would be 'Does switching funds make sense?' or, rather than 'We should have had more money invested in country X', ask 'Do we move money between the countries now?'

Acting on fear

Fear is the emotion felt during a temporary decline. Feeling the fear is called being human; acting on the fear is called being irrational. Fear might make you ask to convert all your investments to cash or similar, as you think that will be safest. Acting on fear is a big mistake, and one that's lurking around every corner for every investor.

Switching your portfolio

As I have stated several times, only switch your investment portfolio if your financial plan has changed, not the other way around. You don't switch an investment portfolio in response to how the markets are behaving at any one point. Trying to time the markets and moving in and out of them usually happens after a decline and through fear. It is madness and it's never been proven to work.

You know how the markets are behaving because your investment portfolio is set up knowing how the markets would behave. Let me repeat: only if your financial plan has changed should you consider if your portfolio should be changed.

Trying to time the market

The conventional wisdom for investment success is to master 'market timings' and to 'select' the right country/sector/company that's going to 'outperform' next (outperform what, who knows?). We see this mindset displayed everywhere, not just within the investment sector but in the wider world too.

How many times have we seen the clichéd depiction of investors and wheeler-dealers yelling 'Sell! Sell! Sell!' into an oversized mobile phone from their corner office in countless Hollywood blockbusters?

However, market timing has never, ever been proven to work. I'll say again: this has never been proven to work. So why on Earth would you seek this for your family and your future generations' life savings?

Thinking you can pick winners in advance or thinking you can pick winners at all is also a fallacy. Assuming you can identify a winning country, company or fund (in advance) after it's done well is like picking race horses after the race – easy in hindsight, proven impossible with foresight. Only inexperienced investors will say, 'Look how well this has done. Why don't we invest in it?'

Trying to time the markets and move in and out of them to make quick money is a mug's game. It often happens after a market decline. If we imagine the markets have declined by 10 or 15 per cent, an inexperienced investor might then say, 'Ah! Should we be coming out of the market now?' The short answer is no. When you try and time the markets, you have two decisions to make. The first is when to come out of the market (eg when the market has declined by -15 per cent). The second decision, which you have to make if you do decide to come out, is when do you go back in?

Very rarely would somebody come out of the market entirely, wait until it has declined by -25 per cent and then get back in. That would be a good move financially, however extremely unlikely that any average investor could pull it off.

You know that if someone is fearful when the market has declined by -15 per cent, if it then declines by -25 per cent they're going to be even more petrified and irrational. What they're likely to do is wait until the markets have come back up and risen to a higher level than it was when they came out of it, and then they're going to get back in. They've had two decisions to make, and it's massively probable they'll get both wrong. They're going to do something called 'selling low and buying high', which is a proven way to go broke in the long term.

Misinformed clients may feel joy in an adviser continually tweaking their portfolio and what they're invested in. The elite adviser knows the only sure indicators of long-term success (performance) are discipline, patience and minimising your investment fees over the long term. Frequently picking outperformers in advance is impossible.

What works is prudent financial planning that creates

financial independence for you and your family – removing the anxiety from money worries, and at the end leaving a meaningful legacy for the people and causes you care about the most. The market will frequently test you with periods of extreme euphoria and then Armageddon, boom and bust, bull and bear. Timing these cycles is near to impossible, so don't try to do it.

Not grasping the role of 'fixed income'
Fixed income is an emotional asset class. During a temporary market decline, having more fixed income (bonds) in your portfolio typically results in smaller losses (temporary declines) compared to being fully invested in global equities. However, in rare and extreme market conditions – occurring perhaps once in a generation – bonds can sometimes perform worse than global equities. While this is highly uncommon, it's important to be aware that it can happen. This very rare phenomenon actually occurred in 2022, when bonds declined much more than global equities.

Grown-up investors have very little (if any) allocated to fixed income. I choose not to invest in fixed-income funds and have no plans to do so in the future. The opportunity cost is simply too high when you compare the long-term returns of fixed income to those of global equities and when you factor in the above inflation returns, the case for bonds declines even further.

However, on the flip side, the more fixed income you have in your portfolio when the market's rising, the less your portfolio is going to rise. What I frequently hear 'cautious' investors say during a temporary decline is, 'I'm not very happy about this decline.' They don't say, 'It's great that I've got 50 per cent of my assets in fixed income, because this temporary decline would have been twice as bad had I had all of my assets in equities.'

They can't intellectualise the role that fixed income plays during a temporary decline in the great companies of the world. But you know differently, and you won't make the same sort of mistakes yourself, especially with this book as a reference for the next time there's a decline.

Taking advice from people who don't have skin in the game

I have skin in the game as I look after my clients' life savings, tell them what to do with them and caringly nudge them on the best course, because I am invested in the exact same portfolios as they are. Financial and money journalists, as well as media personalities, often have the freedom to share tips, opinions and predictions without any accountability for the consequences. They don't have skin in the game, meaning they're not personally impacted by the outcomes of their advice.

I'd always say, if you think they're right, ask them to build you a comprehensive financial plan that maps out all of your goals and the transitions that you want to achieve, serve this financial plan with a historically appropriate global equity/bond portfolio (ideally more equities) and ensure *you* stick to it.

If you think they can build you a personalised financial plan, encourage you to fund it with an appropriate global equity portfolio and ensure you stick to it, then by all means, do exactly what they're telling you to do. They obviously can't do that, because they're sensationalists who are just grabbing eyeballs. By following media tips in your search for 'outperformance' you end up doing the exact opposite – not appreciating that all declines in a globally well-diversified equity portfolio are temporary. And likewise, that the advance, when it continues, is permanent. You need to have a clear understanding of this, and remember that the stock market declines about 25 per cent of the time but increases in value around 75 per cent of the time.

Looking at your portfolio too often

As I mentioned in my list of common investor mistakes above, when the stock market's declining, the more you look at your portfolio valuation, the more you will fill up with financial anxiety. The less you look, the better you do. What you should be seeking is a sense of financial wellbeing.

By addressing your problems and tackling your biases and negative emotions head on, you can be freed from financial anxiety. You've built a financial plan, you've funded it and, with the right behavioural guidance and advice, you can learn to stick to it. You've created the circumstances for a life with the minimum of finance-related stress. If your life changes and your financial plan needs to change too, you can sit down again and adapt it to the new situation.

Losing sight of why you are investing

Most people are investing for a dignified and comfortable retirement, and perhaps to create multi-generational wealth to help out the next generation of their family. It can be easy to lose sight of your long-term aim and give in instead to the pressures and temptations of the here and now – particularly in the heat of a market decline. But if you do that, you won't see the success you want for your family's future. Try to remind yourself of your goal and why you're investing towards it as often as you can.

Stopping your automatic monthly savings contributions when the market temporarily declines

Sometimes people stop, reduce or do not increase their monthly contributions at the same rate during a temporary market decline. This is financial madness. As you are (or working towards) becoming an automatic monthly investor – someone who's paying their future self first by investing every month – when you see red in the investment markets, this is a financial gift. It's when you continue to invest monthly, and ideally increase it to the maximum amount that you can contribute. Why? Because you are buying an asset – the stock market, the great companies of this world – on a monthly basis, and when it's on a temporary sale (in decline), you stock up. Think about it. If you were buying TVs, apples or petrol for a living, when there was a temporary decline (sale) on, you'd go all in. You'd 'load up', as they say.

Realising that a falling stock market is not a bad thing

Everyone enjoys a sale – but not the majority of investors, it seems. When we see sales in every other area of our lives, we rub our hands together and get set to reap the benefits of a dip in prices. Black Friday, Boxing Day, summer sales – all of these are calendar events these days and ones we respond to in a predictably positive way.

So, why should this be different when it comes to a sale in the stock market? If we are invested in the market we tend to just see the negatives of all the red numbers and the declining prices, feeling all the anxiety of this potential (although abstract unless you need to sell your shares today) loss and none of the relish of the potential gains.

But if we are regular investors in the stock market – directing our breakout income into the great companies of the world every month – then we should rejoice at the opportunity it brings because we get more for our money.

Think of it this way. A rising stock market is a declining-in-value market, which means it's getting more and more expensive to buy the same stocks. A declining market means share prices are coming down, so you can get more for your money.

If the market declines significantly one day and your monthly investment goes in the day after, you will be able to buy more shares than the day before. Assuming you are investing for the long term, as you should be, and knowing that the market rises 75 per cent of the time versus a decline at 25 per cent of the time, these shares will recover their value, continue their upward trajectory and you will have more of them. This is the positive side of a declining market – a sale in the stock market – and it's good news for your financial future.

Thinking that you're rational and you make rational choices

I've mentioned rational and irrational behaviour several times so far, but never will you be more tempted to act irrationally with your money than when experiencing a market downturn. Fear really brings out the worst in us and I urge you to re-read this list of mistakes to help you recognise when you might be about to make an irrational decision! Investors also move in cycles. As I've said, the two primary human emotions they move between are fear and greed. They're fearful when the market's declining, and greedy when it's on the way up.

Feeling the fear is perfectly natural, as I discussed earlier, but acting on the fear is irrational and not in anyone's long-term financial interest. You need to remind yourself to sit tight because once the decline is over, the markets will continue to rise.

The market itself is unemotional, but people aren't. Accepting this and making it a part of your relationship with money is vital and, for me, the only real route to providing financial success.

How to prepare for and respond to market crashes (temporary declines)

Crashes and corrections (or market declines, as I'd prefer to call them) are part of investing, but your reaction to them can make or break your long-term financial plans. Here's a story to illustrate what I mean.

Sarah A, now age 60, invested 10 per cent of her income in a diversified stock market portfolio at age 30 and kept increasing her contributions by 0.5 per cent each year. So, 30 years later, she was paying 25 per cent of her income into her portfolio. She forgot her login details, never opened a statement, never reacted to the markets and didn't actually watch the news. She didn't speak to anyone about the economy and she controlled her expenses.

Sarah B, now age 60, started investing at age 30 and was cautious, so only invested 5 per cent of her income to 'see how it went'. She hit some volatility, received stock market tips from her Uncle Jack and read the *Financial Times* at least twice a week as Jack said this was a good idea. She moved in and out of the markets as she saw fit, only increased her contributions when the market did well (buying high) and checked her investment account at least weekly, so she was full of financial anxiety.

On paper, it might seem as if the tuned-in, always-on approach of Sarah B is the correct one, but in terms of your future financial success this couldn't be more wrong. I can't repeat this often enough: invest, forget about it, never look at your account, never research or worry and you will end up beating anyone who obsessively checks and reacts to every market move.

The reason for this is that crashes affect nearly all of us on a behavioural and emotional level, if we allow them to. During temporary declines or market crashes, we are allowed to feel fearful. This is perfectly natural – but acting on that fear is when we make damaging financial mistakes.

The perfect investment portfolio and diversification

The perfect investment portfolio is:

- £ the one you'll stick with through all stock market cycles
- £ has the highest allocation to global equities that you can emotionally stand
- £ if not containing 100 per cent global equities, it contains a sprinkle of global bonds – *if* this means you'll stick with the portfolio.

Most of my clients end up with a portfolio of around 80 per cent global equities. Diversification is the disciplined process by which you assemble your portfolio, with the acknowledgement that you don't know which sectors or countries will outperform the others and which will fade away.

Diversification allows you to capture financial returns across all sectors and geographies and somewhat dampen volatility at any given time. As a simple rule of thumb, you should never own enough of any one thing to make a killing in it. And you should never own enough of any one thing to be killed by it. Diversification is this rule in practice.

Successful investment portfolios should ideally own thousands of individual companies. This could on the face of it appear like the scattergun approach of the uninformed, but it's far from it. It is a wise approach because it aims to broadly capture the returns of the asset class rather than pick individual winners, which is not possible on a regular year-on-year basis.

Avoid the bag of (financial) spanners

As an investment adviser, I see plenty of portfolios that have been created by other investment advisers. Many are dreadful, some consisting of portfolios with more than 50 individual funds and companies, which is utterly pointless naïve complexity – things I don't even recognise, and I've seen a lot of assets in my life.

The reason for the bag of spanners is, you've guessed it, the quest for people to appear smart, to appear sophisticated. But in essence, it's a pointless portfolio that has no direction, stands for nothing, but can justify a big fee. If some of it goes up, as most markets should over time, the money manager will crow that it's a job well done.

Your family's financial fortress should not really contain more than five individual investment funds – and I'm being a bit generous with five. To be honest, you could get away with one. As mentioned under index funds later in this chapter, the 'one fund solution' will allow you to achieve all you wish in regard to your long-term investment returns. But most end consumers don't feel comfortable having their entire life savings in just one fund. Due to this, it's really a personal choice as to how many investment funds you hold. The elegant, simplistic answer is just one, but you'll need to decide how many you'll need to sleep well at night.

The richer you are, the more investment lies you will be told

In all areas of our lives we're told expensive equals better. From handbags to cars to clothes to TVs, received wisdom is the more you spend, the better it will be. But when you apply this rule to your life savings (investing), things change a lot. In this case, the less you pay, the better you'll do, and the simpler your investment portfolio is the more likely it will be that better long-term returns will be achieved.

It can be typical for professional advisers to say things like, 'Oh, for our small-value clients we'll invest in a simple, low-cost index fund, but for our wealthy clients we create bespoke portfolios', or a high-end adviser to say, 'For our smaller clients we use this simpler fund.' What does this mean? That for their bigger clients they overcomplicate things and charge them more?

The data tells us that active management and bespoke portfolios will get left in the dust by a simple index fund invested in the same percentage of growth assets (global equities). So why do the wealthy fall for this every time? I'll tell you why: because they want to feel special, they want the sales tap dance, they want to feel important – and there's no end of investment advisers lining up to sell them the snake oil.

The deca-millionaire won't be sold the same portfolio as the guy who cleans his car, even though the guy who washes the car will likely hammer the deca-millionaire's returns long term – the only time ever when cheap equals pure luxury in all its glory. This is an unvarnished way of saying that, when you have plenty of money, people will pander to you, treat you differently and create elaborate ways to part you with your money for their own benefit.

Imagine the scene. You come into a substantial amount of money and have arranged an appointment with an esteemed and prestigious global bank so that they can open an account for you and look after your investments. You step into the plushly carpeted office, shake hands with the tanned, impeccably suited adviser, nibble on the sumptuous canapés and sip the perfectly chilled fizz they offer throughout your meeting.

They will talk you through the exquisitely complex funds and investment strategies that they have created only for their clients (very exclusive) who have assets above tens of millions at their disposal, list the numbers of team members who will be actively employed to look after your account and will leave you in no doubt you are receiving the all-bells-and-whistles pandering experience. But this whole experience is a lie. In fact, you are wilfully participating in this lie. It's only because potential clients want to be treated in some way differently from the hoi polloi that such banks can get away with it. What you don't see when you're being bamboozled with complicated projections and colourful charts is that you will pay for all of this in the likely high costs that advisers and fund managers at this end of the market will charge you.

Many investors in these situations have no idea of the costs and fees that this level of service comes with, and even less that it is all an exercise in pandering to their need to have their status recognised. Pandering to your ego will cost you a lot when it comes to your life savings. A strong human trait is safety – when it comes to investing, people want safe and not cheap.

Of course, it's important to treat clients well and provide a good service, but not one that is so expensive it starts to contradict the very purpose of financial advice! The nature of money or the principles of good advice don't change depending on the amount of it that you have. If you think it does, someone is lying to you.

Asset classes

There are four key asset classes that you need to be aware of:

- £ cash
- £ fixed income
- £ equities
- £ property.

Although there are other asset classes – commodities, alternatives, hedge funds and private equity, to name a few – these four are the important ones you need to know about.

Cash refers to cash deposited in a current or savings account in the bank, not invested money. This is useful for monthly cash flow and any known expenditure you have in the near term, such as purchasing a car or a house. This won't produce the best return; its ready availability is its greatest asset.

Fixed income is lending your money to governments and companies. It is split between government bonds (lent to governments) and corporate bonds (lent to companies). As the name suggests, you are paid a fixed income over the time you loan the funds to these organisations.

As an asset class, fixed income is more of an emotional asset class than financial (see 'Not grasping the role of fixed income' in market decline mistakes above). By this I mean if you are not comfortable with the risk (volatility) associated with equities, fixed income provides a more stable option and smoother ride than going all in on equities.

Investing in **equities** is the act of buying an ownership stake (even if it is very small) in the great businesses of the world, the brands we all know and recognise. This is a higher volatility option than fixed income but is where superior long-term reward comes from. It's a trade-off between volatility and reward.

Investing in **property** as an asset class means investing in physical property, ie bricks and mortar rather than property funds. It is a mini-business in itself, which comes with its own responsibilities and concerns. I'm pro property investing and buying physical properties that you own as long as you're aware of the 'high hassle factor'.

Avoid any other flavour of property investing, be it funds, syndicates or collective schemes, because they all turn out to be terrible. As a professional adviser I see a lot of fraud committed in property-related schemes because the schemes are easy to sell, and a fool and their money are easily parted!

As a regulated financial adviser, I can't tell you which funds to invest in.

Productive investment asset classes

For an asset to find a place in your family's financial fortress, it needs to be a productive asset class. For an asset class to be productive, it needs to produce an income. My definition goes a little further: not only does the asset need to produce income, it needs to provide a rising income. For an asset to be deemed a real asset, it needs to produce a natural rising income. The only two assets that do this are businesses and physical property.

Global businesses can be accessed by investing in a global equity investment fund. The great wonder of the stock market is that we all get the opportunity to buy into the great businesses of this world whenever we want to, and have access to the returns they provide by investing in global equities. Investing in equities is a vote of confidence in human endeavour and in the future.

I have faith that humans will continue to produce products and services that other humans will want to buy far into the future and companies will grow and increase in value on the back of these well-established and historically provable human instincts. Yes, there will be some ups and downs along the way; there must be. But, over time, investing in equities, driven by human ingenuity and human demand, will deliver a return to those who invest in the great companies in the world. We have seen repeatedly that the dividends and the profits that these companies produce have outpaced inflation over multiple decades, and because of rising profits this then results in a rise in capital value.

Property, too, is a proven way to see a return on your investment. This means physical property that you can see, touch and rent out to people or businesses. It doesn't include options such as loaning money to property developers, or anything peripheral to the property sector. It's about bricks and mortar only.

The only property investing I'm a fan of is you owning the physical property, you being the landlord. Most people put property into the high-hassle, high-friction bucket and avoid it. I am a landlord and have owned various investment properties. It works, but it is a load of hassle and in the long term, investing in global equities is more enjoyable, less hassle and more lucrative. However, as with investing in businesses, historical data shows us that both rents and the capital value of properties have increased over time, meaning again that they pass the smell test as an asset providing a rise in income and in capital value.

If physical property is not your thing and it's too much hassle, the only option is to invest your family's financial fortress into global equities, the only truly passive option. The long-term returns from global equities are fantastic, albeit with some deep temporary declines (see the index funds section below).

Most asset classes fail the rising income test, so they have little or no place in your family's financial fortress. As a result of a real asset providing rising income, over time its capital value will increase. Contrast this with other popular investment options that sometimes catch the investor's eye. Take gold, for example, which is an asset that many investors run to in times of uncertainty. Gold may rise in capital value, but it does not produce a rising income. It costs you to store it and its long-term return over 100 years has been pitiful – but there's always someone ready to sell you the shiny useless stuff. Investing in art may also see a rise in capital value, but it won't provide you with any sort of income.

Fixed income fails the real asset test because, as the name confirms, it produces a fixed income and not a rising one. Keeping your assets in cash doesn't satisfy the criteria either. If it doesn't pass the investment smell test, it's not worthy of your family's long-term investable assets.

Business, bricks and cash

The only three financial assets that I own are these:

- £ businesses
- £ bricks
- £ cash.

I own my own businesses, but more importantly I invest in thousands of elite global businesses via the global equity funds I hold. I not only hold them, I aggressively contribute too. I own my own house and have a few investment properties. If being a landlord is not your game, then you'll likely just own your own home. Cash is the final asset I hold – for cashflow reasons in my businesses and for personal lifestyle cashflow outside my businesses. Any additional cash is invested in businesses via global equity funds.

You only need these three to build all the wealth and happiness in your financial life. You don't *need* to 'diversify' across other types of asset. If you choose to stick with these three, you'll have a simple, perfectly set-up financial life.

Index funds – the one-fund solution

Broadly speaking, there are two types of investment strategy. The first is known as active investing, where you try to pick winning companies or sectors and outsmart the rest of the stock market participants, while they try to do the same to you and everyone else. The evidence, however, tells us that over multiple decades it is hard for active managers to comfortably beat their own self-imposed benchmark of financial success that they are trying to outperform.

The alternative approach is passive investing, which simply tracks the stock market index that active managers aim to outperform, seeking to just match its returns. As very few active managers can beat their index long term, and as the passive investor is trying to replicate the said index, the passive investor becomes the outperformer over the long term.

What drives the global stock markets long term is a handful of companies that absolutely fly, shooting the lights out as it were. But the problem is you never know with foresight which companies these will be – with hindsight it's clear as day!

To combat this, you just buy the market via an index fund, and whatever company/sector or latest trend is rising aggressively, you own it – you own the haystack and you're not looking for needles. On the flip side, owning an index fund also means you'll own companies that'll die, but you don't care, because new ones will come along and, anyway, you still own the ones that will fly. Fly or die, you don't care.

So when you hear about the latest company to have tripled in the last year, you can smile, because you'll own a tiny slice of it and the biggest individual company in the index will likely be your biggest single holding and you own it by accident due to just owning all the companies.

Index (passive) investing replicates the performance of a specific index, such as the FTSE100 or the S&P 500. An index fund is an investment that follows a specific stock market index (a list of all the companies trading on that stock market). It invests in all the companies in that index, giving you broad exposure to the market. It's low cost, easy to manage, and aims to match the market's performance over time. You can buy global equity funds for very little. In the US, decent index funds that will do everything you want them to do can be bought for as little as 0.02 per cent per annum, as close to 'free' as you can get.

In the UK, I see one-fund solutions for around 0.12 per cent per annum, a lot more than they are in the US, but still very low cost.

The costs mentioned here can be framed as 'basically free'. You can build wealth and create economic freedom for you and your family at basically no (tiny) cost.

Do you recall the financial robot vs human emotion experiment from Chapter 3? What would be the right answer for your family's financial fortress: invest in one fund or many? A financial robot would invest in one fund, never regret their robot decision and never have any remorse as they know this is the right action to take financially.

A human, on the other hand, finds it hard during market declines to be absolutely convinced that the one fund is the right answer, so I have found with the humans I look after that it helps them sleep slightly better at night to have their life savings invested across a few funds (see above), even though the financial robot who makes perfectly optimal decisions would likely not do this. The best portfolio is the one you'll stick with, so spend some time thinking about how many funds you'd be comfortable having in your long-term serious money portfolio.

It's often said that buying an index fund is buying into average returns. This was a mantra I followed early in my career. I used to think it was better to accept consistent average returns rather than try to find above-average returns and risk ending up below average.

It seemed safer to 'guarantee' an average return than to take a chance on achieving above-average performance. However, I've since realised that this concept of indexing being average is totally and utterly wrong. There's some truth in the statement, but it's a weak truth. Let me explain why. Traditionally, it is thought that if you buy the index fund, you're buying average performance. This is correct if you are looking at a short time frame; however, every year you own the index fund, it becomes an outperformer against its peers. The outperformance is predominantly based on the lower fees you are paying but another huge factor is down to owning the companies that fly over long periods. Buying the index is far from average over the long term.

In the first year, owning an index fund compared to other funds will give you approximately 'average' returns, but thinking in a one-year time horizon is insanely shortsighted. Long-term investing spans decades, and you should default to a 30-year time horizon. Thinking in 30-year chunks (as a minimum) is how the smart investor thinks. Even if you're, say, 80 years of age, if your lifestyle spending needs are covered, then any capital/money you have invested is now likely going to be passed down.

Even an 80-year-old should think long term, with 30 years being a simple marker. Obviously if you're 35 and just starting your investing mission, you should ideally be thinking way longer than 30 years ahead, because no one knows what the future holds, how long you'll live and how much money you'll be passing down to the people and causes you care about.

If you own an index fund versus an active fund over this long-term period, you gradually become a small outperformer as each year rolls on. Imagine a league table with 100 funds, and your index fund is one of them. In the first year, you're in position 50 out of 100. In the second year, you nudge up to 48 out of 100. In the third year, you move to 46 out of 100, and so on. By year ten, hypothetically, you'll be around position 30 out of 100, climbing up the league table bit by bit, year by year.

In year 30, you could be close to position 1 out of 100. For balance, let's assume three exceptional fund managers are ahead of you due to luck and/or skill, so you'll settle for position 4 out of 100. This is not average. It starts off average, but with patience and time, you end up 'winning' the investment game. Index investing is winning investing and far from average. Even professionals don't always understand this, so if you've grasped this concept, you're well on your way to investment literacy.

Grasping this concept is so important, I suggest you read this section again if it's not yet landed with you, because being an owner of index funds should fill you with joy knowing that in the long run you'll be the investing winner, which means you've achieved the highest on-average multi-decade returns.

Asset class index investing will likely beat 90 per cent of your neighbours' investments if you stick to it for one decade or more. After multiple decades, you'll beat 99 per cent of them. Each year an index fund is owned, it incrementally outperforms its peers.

You'll always own the beasts

If you don't follow investment news, you would have missed a rather staggering story in 2024. In June of that year, a relatively unknown company, NVIDIA, became the biggest listed company in the world. Yes, that's right, it overtook both Apple and Microsoft to claim the top slot.

Launched in 1993, the company's main product is the graphics processing units (GPUs) traditionally used in gaming computers. In 2001, its steady growth resulted in it entering the S&P 500 by replacing Enron. The real growth, however, only started in the past few years when its products became sought after for mining cryptocurrency and, more recently, for powering the new wave of artificial intelligence (AI) engines.

Its growth since 2019 has been staggering. In 2019, NVIDIA traded at $4 per share. At one point in June 2024, the share price was $126. Naturally, much media coverage has fixated on the remarkable wealth investors could have made by picking to invest in NVIDIA stock before its rise in popularity. However, smart investors know that predicting which companies will become these market leaders is incredibly difficult. With hindsight, it seems obvious – how could Amazon not be huge; how could Tesla not be a 'big beast'?

Stock picking can be risky, often leading to missed opportunities and heightened anxiety. If you didn't own NVIDIA directly, there's likely no need to despair. If you are invested in a global equity fund, you likely already own NVIDIA shares. As an investor, nothing could be better news: owning a global equity fund that tracks an index like the S&P 500 (or other large index) means you'll always own the shares of the biggest companies.

As companies like NVIDIA rise to dominance, they

are promptly included in these indices, guaranteeing their presence in your investment portfolio. NVIDIA, for example, would have been held since 2001.

Companies that make the news for exponential growth almost always experience periods where they lose more than half of their value over short periods of time. For example, in 2022 Amazon lost close to 60 per cent of its market value while the market as a whole only declined 25 per cent.

A global fund gives you the growth exposure of the stocks that fly while also giving you the protection of a diversified portfolio. As a result, you won't need to worry about missing out on the next big thing. Whether it's an emerging tech giant or a company revolutionising an industry, being part of a diversified global equity fund ensures you're always in the mix.

You can ignore the noise

While the above good news seems common sense, you'll seldom read about it in the financial media. Growing wealth slowly over time does not make for exciting headlines. A story about the latest stock to explode makes for a better story, which is why you will always wonder if you're losing out to others.

There are numerous reasons to own index funds, and data from Saxo Group shows that they tend to outperform actively managed funds over meaningful periods, but one key advantage of index funds is that they always include the market's dominant companies. It's impossible to predict which sector will dominate the top ten spots, but the good news is you don't need to guess because you'll own a small slice of it regardless. Some stocks die, some stocks fly and some stocks really soar.

Trying to pick these winners in advance is a fool's errand. By owning a broad global equity fund, you'll be a part owner in the market's dominant companies, even those no one could predict with foresight. This approach allows you to benefit from the growth of these giants without the stress and uncertainty of trying to pick individual winners.

You're swapping money for financial independence investment units. An effective and sane way to approach investing is to focus on the number of fund units (literally, the number of units of the fund) you own rather than the daily fluctuations of your portfolio's value. You are buying units, not prices.

Each additional unit you purchase, whether through lump-sum investments or regular contributions, is a building block in your journey toward financial independence. Think of it as exchanging money for financial independence units, a process you ideally continue indefinitely.

As I have stated repeatedly above – and probably will again – a wise investor resists emotional reactions during periods of fear or greed and understands that market cycles are inevitable.

Wise investors build their financial future unit by unit, staying focused on the big picture, appreciating both phases of the cycle and viewing all cycles positively. A market decline provides you with the rare opportunity to buy more units for every pound (or dollar) you're investing, and at a faster rate. This is because the unit price has declined, which as a result means you're buying more units per amount invested.

A rising market boosts your progress towards independence by making your units more valuable. If the item that your future financial independence depends on is on sale, should you be happy or sad?

Would you buy more or stop buying for a while until the price increases again? If you're investing for a lifetime, mindset is everything.

Investment lifeboat drills

The best time to do a lifeboat drill is when the sea is calm and you're in port. Don't wait until the wind is getting up, the sea swell is increasing and the waves are rising. In investing, this means thinking your strategy through in advance of stock market volatility (usually declines). It is about understanding and anticipating that markets will sometimes have long periods of negativity and a downward direction.

Let's explore what this means and how to do it. The benefit of doing a lifeboat drill before you hit the proverbial iceberg is so that you won't panic when something goes wrong. Regularly reviewing your portfolios (with your adviser, if you have one) ensures that they're still appropriate for your level of risk tolerance.

Each portfolio will behave differently when there's a 'storm' because of how it's been set up. So make sure you understand how your own portfolio might behave (respond) when a storm hits. It's also good to have a fund pot to cover any expenses you might face during a downturn – that way you can avoid selling stocks during the crisis just to liquidate some money.

Indeed, having that savings pot to fall back on will protect you even if you haven't really paid attention to a market downturn until you're in the middle of it. Just remember – don't make any sudden decisions and sell off your stocks. That won't help.

5

Partnering and finding support

I sometimes think of the role of the financial adviser as being like that of a doctor: the doctor writes medical prescriptions for their patients; the financial adviser writes financial prescriptions for their clients. When a new client walks into my office, I often say, 'I know your financial prescription. Now please tell me what's wrong with you.'

It sounds crazy to think that a financial adviser would be able to make such an instant diagnosis of a client's condition without an examination or discussion of their symptoms. But when it comes to financial and investing success, the prescription is always the same, even if the doses vary. And what is the prescription? Clear all crappy debt, spend less than you earn, invest the difference correctly, work from a fluid financial plan.

How a good financial adviser can help you

As a rule, financial advice doesn't take enough account of emotions and behaviour, but this is fundamental to long-term success. Human behaviour is the biggest potential eroder of the value of your investments.

Having now spent nearly two decades advising clients about money decisions, I know making successful financial plans and high-level financial decisions cannot be done successfully without assistance. I'm not the first to come to this conclusion, but investing success is less to do with knowledge and more to do with how an individual makes decisions in high-pressure, high-impact environments.

If we could get all the clients of financial advisers together from all over the world and ask them what they pay their advisers for, we would get as many different answers as individuals. However, most of them would include some reference to money or finances. They might also mention their retirement plan or their investment portfolio or whatever their trigger was for looking for a financial adviser in the first place. I can tell you one sentence that wouldn't come out of the mouths of any of them and that's: 'I'm paying my adviser to protect me from myself and ensure I don't sabotage my own life plans.'

People will talk about 'optimising' their investments or ask what's the 'best' pension product 'at the moment' as if these issues should be their focus rather than thinking of what an adviser provides as more like a doctor–patient relationship, which should be far closer to the reality.

Most of what my clients think they are paying me for – investment management and financial advice – I actually feel as if I'm doing for free. With advances in technology, it's rapidly heading towards being free in the future anyway.

This bit is straightforward and, after many years as a financial adviser, my experience means I have seen similar examples and recognise what my clients need quite easily. In contrast to this, every single individual, in terms of their behaviour, attitudes, background and experience of money, is different.

Behavioural coaching is so crucial to financial life

success that the other parts of an adviser's job are almost incidental. If you asked me to put a percentage on it, I'd say 30 per cent of my efforts are spent on the strategy and the remaining 70 per cent is directed to behavioural coaching. A financial plan without the coaching alongside it is pointless.

I understand that there are issues at play here. Money is a difficult topic to talk about. We don't like discussing personal circumstances with a stranger; it seems complicated; we don't want to look stupid or feel embarrassed.

One of the most frustrating things is that people often do want to seek advice, but they're aware that they lack knowledge on the subject of investing. Alongside that, they worry that a financial adviser may take advantage of that fact. They expect the adviser to make things more complicated than they are, charge them huge fees and not deliver the promised results.

If you're looking for a financial adviser, then please do your due diligence. Ask for recommendations from people you trust. You can also use a website such as Citizens Advice – they even have a facility for you to check how a financial service measures up (see References for full details).

It's not just clients who think it's all about a focus on finance; many advisers think they still manage money too, rather than managing and supporting the people who have it. A good financial adviser will always be alert to their clients' tendency to make the wrong decision, starting off on the route to bad behaviour. A poor financial adviser will only focus on managing money.

How to spot a poor financial adviser

As I've said, there are ways to do due diligence before you sign on to work with an adviser. A good one always has your best interests at heart and will talk through the pros and cons of not only investment decisions but behaviours around your portfolio.

For example, a client may ask to see the performance of 'XYZ fund' over the past year. A poor financial adviser might simply hand over the information. A good adviser, however, will explain why that's not a good idea. That's because they know that the performance of any fund over a year-to-year measure will not give an accurate reading or prediction of the investor's lifetime financial success.

A good adviser is there to serve as a partner on your financial journey, and that means sometimes they say things you don't want to hear. They have to point out financial misbehaviour every time it happens so that you can make the best possible decisions for your money. So, while the client may insist on having that information on XYZ fund, their adviser will share it with a large note of caution and gently encourage them to see the bigger picture.

Expectations for financial advice

It's good to be clear and upfront about what financial advice can provide and, perhaps more importantly, what it can't. Often, what financial advice can't do is what people initially seek from financial advisers, and it's important that you're clear on what financial advice can't do from the beginning.

What financial advice can do

Good financial advice gets to know you, your hopes, fears, goals and aspirations. It sketches out a plan for your financial future and funds it with a well-crafted portfolio. A good adviser will be a caring, considerate sounding board for all your major (or minor) life decisions and provide clarity about the confusing world of wealth creation. Good financial advice removes the anxiety you feel about being financially disorganised and helps you avoid the 'big mistakes'. You can be optimistic during periods of major pessimism, and a good adviser will help you manage your money in the same way we manage our own.

Financial advisers will also help reduce the amount of tax you pay and promote great financial behaviour for your future financial success. They also give advice on regulations and any laws you need to abide by, and how this applies depending on which country you live in.

What financial advice can't do

Financial advisers cannot predict the future. Most people want us to predict the future, such as the short-term performance of the stock market, the direction of the economy and this year's hot companies for portfolio picks. No one can do this. History is our only guide as there are no facts about the future. A typical investor is very short-term focused, but great financial advisers are long-term planners, and over the long term the markets will produce fabulous returns, as they have done in the past over long periods.

Financial advisers who take a financial planning approach, rather than focusing solely on investments, won't manage your portfolio in isolation. Instead, they'll ensure any investment decisions are guided by a clear financial plan that reflects your full financial picture.

We also don't manage half your investment account and allow the rest to be managed elsewhere – an army general would never manage half an army. Your portfolio is central to and funds your financial plan. Similarly, we cannot help to provide high returns with low volatility as this is not possible.

We can't pick the correct time to invest – we believe in 'time in' the market and not 'timing' the market. The best time to invest was years ago; the second best time is today.

Finally, and importantly, we can't allow you to do anything we wouldn't do ourselves. We're always on the alert for spotting any financially destructive behaviour.

We need to talk
Finding a good financial adviser

Our society is full of divisions, but nothing divides people like money. Complexity in the way we talk about money scares people off, keeps them out of the conversation or restricts their understanding. Call it what you like – elitism, snobbery or just bad communication – it needs to change.

We all need to address the way we communicate financial ideas and concepts. Democratising financial advice and making it accessible to all is something I am particularly passionate about. I'm passionate about it because it is extremely important to all of us.

I want you to feel empowered to take control of your financial decisions and financial future, and give you the confidence and self-belief that this is an opportunity that's available to you. I want you to start thinking about financial advice and investment success as something you can obtain, albeit with some focused work.

It should be as normal a part of your life as going to the dentist or getting the car serviced. You should think of investment management as a basic instrumental process, not a high-end indulgence – as glamorous as getting the car serviced but no less essential. Ideally, I would like you to join me in embracing my behavioural approach to managing money, and spread the word to your family, friends and colleagues!

The ability to create wealth or build financial independence for ourselves should be an opportunity open to everyone. Access to good financial advice ought to be universal, but until we start putting it on the curriculum in schools those of us in the financial advice profession must invite as many people as possible inside our virtual classrooms, spreading the word as best we can.

Alongside being a financial adviser, I see myself as a communicator. It's my job to communicate effectively about money and financial ideas. Understanding your financial circumstances clearly, as well as the opportunities you have and the risks of not engaging with financial decisions, is crucial for your long-term wellbeing.

It's easy to make financial communication technical and complex. It's harder and takes much more time to simplify it and make it accessible to you, to everyone – but the onus really is on me and my fellow financial advisers to do just that. The language we use and the way we communicate should include, not exclude, people and make the subject accessible to everyone.

An adviser who communicates with jargon that is only understood by other financial people is wrong. This is a trait you should avoid when seeking a good financial adviser to guide you and your family.

When you look for the right independent financial adviser (IFA) for you, there are a couple of trusted websites that you can rely on. First, a legitimate IFA has to be registered with the Financial Conduct Authority. They maintain a register where you can check any adviser you're considering working with. You can also find an IFA in your local area via the MoneyHelper website (see References for full details).

I'm not saying we should get rid of jargon completely or from all areas. It's useful to use it within the profession to discuss technical issues where necessary, but financial advisers need to be mindful of jargon and adopt new principles when talking to everyday investors.

The medical profession might use Latin or technical terms among themselves, but they don't employ them to explain what's happening to you because they want you to understand your situation and help you to get better. Financial advice should be no different.

I'm on a mission to change this and I certainly always seek to use simpler, more straightforward language at every opportunity. I've trained a number of advisers over the years who are starting to use my terminology too, which is encouraging and hopefully useful and effective for their clients.

Visit Mavenadviser.com to find out more about what I do. I also have a podcast archive of 300 episodes packed with value, and a blog full of helpful articles (check the References section for full details).

What's causing the communication breakdown?

Here are some of my observations on what makes a poor financial adviser:

- £ Laziness – it's difficult and time consuming to think through some of these concepts and to make them accessible to a mainstream audience.
- £ A bid to 'impress' clients – baffling you with jargon to make an impression – and money. As noted in the previous chapter, there are practitioners in the financial services industry who say what people want to hear or rely on sales patter and marketing speak for their living.
- £ Overcomplicating for profit – people who work in money sometimes try to make what they do seem complicated. The reason for this is that the person on the street doesn't like the answer to be easy and may be less inclined to pay for an easy solution.

- £ Salespeople go through the motions of making it look complicated so that they look as if they earn their money. Competence isn't rewarded in this instance. Complexity sells.
- £ Deception – we live in a wicked world where outright deception and misinformation is employed to con or scam people out of their money.

The value and cost of investment management

For some time I have witnessed the rise of 'robo' advice and solutions. These are currently just super-cheap online investment management platforms where there may be some custodian fees and a small management fee.

They don't charge for advice as they currently don't offer any. This situation has contributed significantly to the growing perception that now all investment management should be as near to free and as stripped down in terms of cost as possible, with frictionless access to the markets.

It's worth looking into this more closely.

The arrival of 'robo advice' has been the most talked-about topic for some time now by all areas of the financial press. The media focus is on how human advisers are being displaced, or 'disrupted', by machines and it's asking whether traditional, old-fashioned financial advisers will become a thing of the past as we all stand aside for the march of AI.

However, these advocates and evangelists for the DIY investment culture have lied to investors. They have convinced them they can easily manage their family's financial future single handed and without a professional as long as they know their way around an app or two on their smartphone or a platform on their laptop. The truth is: they can't.

The huge majority of people are unlikely to have the

level of experience and knowledge that's required to create a financial plan – or, more importantly, the wisdom and discipline to stick to it to ensure they react appropriately at every financial crossroads for the rest of their lives.

However, not all clients are willing to take advice. They may be overconfident in their abilities and have had some positive reinforcement of the actions they have already taken. They may have picked some funds that have done well, read about financial rules online and so on.

The main appeal of DIY investing for many is the perception that it's cheaper than using a financial adviser, which on the surface may seem true. However, what many don't realise is that this decision could cost them significantly more in the long run.

A piece of broad-brush advice that will be useful in many areas of your financial life, but will also apply when you're seeking a financial adviser, is the idiom 'look after the pennies and the pounds will look after themselves', meaning if you don't waste small amounts of money, it will accumulate capital.

Looking to save on financial advice when you venture into investing is not going to help the pounds look after themselves, or multiply, or build some financial security for you and your loved ones. Solid advice from a good financial adviser is a must.

Let me give you an example. Even the most novice and inexperienced of investors will understand that, when it comes to investing, selling low and buying high is the worst possible long-term strategy. Agreed? Good.

Now, when the result of the Brexit referendum was announced in 2016, I noticed that most of the large DIY investing platforms had brought in extra staff over the weekend to deal with the 'increased demand'. This need for more hands on deck was generated by DIY investors seeking to sell and move their investments from stocks and shares into cash after a sharp decline in the market in response to the referendum result.

Let's look closer at this strategy. The DIY investors were selling their portfolios after a decline had happened. They panicked and sold at a temporary bottom when the shares were low in value. They then likely waited until a recovery when the market was high again and bought back the same shares.

So, if a portfolio of, say, £100k takes a temporary decline to £95k and the investor sells, then waits until a recovery occurs and buys back in when it is 10 per cent higher, this would have actually cost them 10 per cent. A panicked reaction to a temporary decline and literally waiting until the market has got more expensive again would have cost the client £10k in this case.

If they'd had an adviser on hand, the adviser would have told them to simply sit tight and do nothing at all. If the adviser charged their fee as a percentage (say 1 per cent a year) of assets under management (translating to £1k per annum) they would have saved them £9k in seconds.

Or, looking at it another way, that's ten years' worth of advisers' fees by saying two words: 'Do nothing.' In investment terms, paying £1,000 for £10,000 worth of advice is one of the best returns you'll ever get.

You need to remember that robo platforms only sell access to the markets. That's all. They don't care what else is going on in your life, what your broader goals are, nor do they have any understanding of your biases when it comes to money.

Robo platforms powered by algorithms can't coach humans out of bad, self-destructive decisions that work against their long-term goals for themselves and their families. The difference between behavioural advice and an online platform is that advisers sell wisdom – which is a rare commodity, and not one on offer from an online platform.

Technology will keep developing and advancing, and automation will definitely continue to play an increasing role in investment management, speeding up processes, making advisers more efficient in time and effort on everyday tasks, but it can't solve all problems and needs to be balanced by a human approach that accounts for emotional and irrational idiosyncrasies.

Humans are complex creatures, and financial advice and solutions need to address this – which means having other humans provide considered coaching and advice, not giving up this privileged position to an algorithm.

Going forward, the value of financial advice will come from financial strategy and behavioural coaching. These will become the core offering of financial advisers as these aspects are very difficult to automate. This means helping you stay committed to your financial plan and understand the bigger picture.

Lifelong advice for a long life

If human beings came with an expiry date attached, the financial adviser role would be a lot easier. Human insurance is crucial (see Chapter 3) because an untimely death could cause a family to face financial ruin. However if a death date was known, you could know with more certainty the amount of money you'd need for the rest of your life, although of course you can't predict inflation fluctuations.

Financial planning is about striking a fine balance between enjoying life while you're living it and at the same time squirrelling away some money for your unknown future. The reason the financial advice profession works the way it does is because we don't know how long we'll end up being on this planet.

We need to prepare for every eventuality along the way to the ultimate eventuality, whenever that might be. When I'm helping my clients to plan, I tell them that their financial master plan will assume they will live until they are 100.

Most of them protest that they don't think they'll get anywhere near this grand old age, but I tell them they might and it's my job to help them prepare for this possibility, however remote (in both senses) it might seem. The aim is to stop people from compromising their future selves by misbehaving today – whatever ultimate age they achieve.

Even if I'm wrong, I'd rather err on the side of a comfortable and fulfilling later life. I'd prefer your money to live far longer than you, rather than your money expiring before you do, leaving you to live out your last years broke.

For me, going through this exercise with clients really brings it home to them, and always reminds me of how good financial planning really does mean a plan for your entire life. Every day we encourage people to look further ahead in their lives than anyone else would ever ask them to because we care about how their future is going to turn out.

If they are lucky, there will be many steps and transitions along the way in a fulfilling and enjoyable life. First job, buying a house, getting married, having a family, starting and selling a business, retiring and leaving a legacy.

And, of course, while the financial plan is tailored to the individual doing the investing, I always take into account their personal life – partner, children and other dependants. The plan takes into consideration what will happen after the client dies, as well as where the money to invest is coming from. I always make sure that the client I make the plan for has the full support of their partner and they know that money is being invested for a better family future.

An adviser's job is to anticipate these transitions in life, first making them possible and then making them as smooth as possible when they're happening. We give advice and guidance today that is consistent with the goals and ambitions for the rest of your life.

Investment trends and financial advice fashions might change, which is why an annual planning review of your financial plan is so important, but people and their lives will always be at the heart of good, effective financial planning.

The end of the book... but the start of a better financial journey

Congratulations! You've reached the end of the book. Now you know what to do to move away from financial naivety and towards building a better, financially stable future for you and your family.

This book is intended to be a resource for you to refer back to, particularly when you're worried about market fluctuations or declines. When that happens, read the sections about the markets again, and you'll be reassured. DON'T make any sudden decisions!

I've explored what to think about when you start investing, the importance of having insurance and pensions and how a financial adviser can help you (so long as you've done your due diligence to find a good one).

My six key principles in Chapter 2 will help you to get your finances back on track so that you know what you have to work with when you start investing. Alongside them, my ten commandments for investing in Chapter 4 will give you the clear steps to take to invest your money wisely. And the section 'Disciplined behaviour will ensure your financial success' in Chapter 4, which covers behavioural biases, will be a good reference for you when you're trying to avoid making bad financial decisions.

Remember that you're a human, not a robot! You will make mistakes, but they'll be less common when you understand where your behaviours are coming from.

Bonus section

I have condensed my 20 years of experience in the money game into a five-minute message. Enjoy.

The five-minute money message

- £ Being born poor is no one's fault, but dying poor is. We have to take personal responsibility; we have to grow up and become financially literate. It's a journey, a long journey; it's not easy, but why should it be easy?
- £ Money is the story you tell yourself, as are most things in life. Stop carrying negative money stories around, because no one really cares.
- £ You should know how many months you have left in your wealth window: your wealth window is from now until you stop receiving an earned income. For example, my wealth window is 264 months, 263, 262... You should always express your wealth window in months, because years sound like an eternity.
- £ You have two important stages in life: your saving stage (aka your wealth window) and then your spending stage, aka retirement. All other traditional life stages are really transitions, which are ongoing and fluid.

- £ Life's a balance between enjoying 'now' and planning for 'then'.
- £ Don't ever think you'll make money through financial trading (FX, commodities) or any other flavour of this form of gambling. The people who make money are the trading training companies and the financial bookmakers, and the loser rates are off the charts. They rely on new blood (also known as mugs) coming through, frequently middle-aged men with excess income and excess egos, who think, 'Surely I can beat the odds!' No, you can't. Grow up.
- £ Stick to the wealth creation strategies that have always worked. This means either setting up your own business or, if you are an employee, investing in all the other great businesses (the stock market). Poor people save, rich people INVEST.
- £ The other wealth vehicle that has always worked is investing in physical property, which I call bricks. The only way to create real wealth is investing in businesses or bricks, as both provide a rising income and rising capital values over multiple decades, which we know if we use history as our guide.
- £ Asset class index investing will likely beat 90 per cent of your neighbours if you stick to it for one decade or more. After multiple decades you'll beat 99 per cent of them; each year an index fund is owned, it incrementally outperforms its peers. It's basic maths, which few seem to want to understand.
- £ Once a globally diversified index fund portfolio has been purchased, never ever sell it. It'll always be a mistake and it'll always be *your* mistake. A permanent loss in a globally well-diversified equity portfolio is a human achievement of which the market is incapable.
- £ Maximise your pensions at work and benefit from

your employer's maximum matched contribution. This is FREE MONEY and it's rare. If you run your own business, get investing now and invest more than you think possible. You're way behind the employees, trust me.

- £ Ideally, invest your age as the percentage of your net income: at age 30, invest 30 per cent of your net income and at age 45, invest 45 per cent. Most people can't do this, me included. As a minimum default think 20 per cent of your take-home net pay.
- £ Investing today is the spending tomorrow of YOUR future self, and so your future self should be your biggest monthly bill; more than your mortgage and certainly more than your holidays and cars.
- £ Ideally, increase your top line – your income. If you can't, your only financial option is to reduce your bottom line, which is your expenses. Lifestyle creep is way more pervasive than we all think.
- £ Most people make financial decisions as a result of what happens close to them.
- £ Credit cards can be helpful during periods of your life, but it's best not to use them. If you use credit cards to maintain an expensive lifestyle to impress people you barely know, this is the biggest financial mistake you'll make and you deserve all you get financially. Delayed gratification is one of the most mature money skills a person can have.
- £ Insure yourself against bad surprises, whether that's being hit by a car or developing a serious illness such as cancer or having a heart attack or a stroke. If you don't, when you most need it, you'll be uninsurable.
- £ Most people set up insurances as a consequence of some devastating personal news about a friend or a loved one. It is what it is. You hope all your insurance

premiums are an utter waste of money – I know I do – but I know this game well.
- £ Know that you are and always have been the biggest wealth destroyer of all, and then learn to not be. Becoming wise about your money will be the best gift you can give yourself.
- £ Financial literacy is a superpower.
- £ Buy cheap, buy twice.
- £ Great financial advice is not a cost, it's an investment. Those advisers are between you and all your decisions, and that's invaluable.
- £ Tax is likely your biggest expense, so learn how to control its impact and also be happy that you have or will have large tax bills. It means you're doing well and you should frame tax as a good thing.
- £ The stock market (the great businesses of the world) rewards the patient and punishes the rest.
- £ Mistakes of omission (as in, things you didn't do, usually due to fear) have more impact long term than mistakes of action (mistakes you actually made).
- £ Learn from the mistakes of others.

References

Chapter 3

The 4 per cent rule: investopedia.com/terms/f/four-percent-rule.asp

Workplace pensions rules: www.gov.uk/employers-workplace-pensions-rules; gov.uk/workplace-pensions/what-you-your-employer-and-the-government-pay

The FIRE movement: investopedia.com/terms/f/financial-independence-retire-early-fire.asp

Chapter 4

Decker, M (2023) 'Four historical patterns in the markets for investors to know'. Kiplinger, 4 December. URL: kiplinger.com/investing/historical-stock-market-patterns-for-investors-to-know

Waymire, M M (2016) 'A fly-by history of behavioral finance'. Nasdaq, 15 August. URL: nasdaq.com/articles/fly-history-behavioral-finance-2016-08-15

DALBAR Quantitative Analysis of Investor Behaviour report, qaib.com

Capital.com 'New research: Success is limited until DIY investors break bad habits'. URL: ft.com/partnercontent/capital-com/new-research-success-is-limited-until-diy-investors-break-bad-habits.html

Merrill Lynch 'Quiz: What's your true risk tolerance?' URL: ml.com/articles/risk-tolerance-quiz.html

Munger, C (1994) Speech to the USC Business School: 'A lesson on elementary worldly wisdom as it relates to investment management & business'. URL: fs.blog/great-talks/a-lesson-on-worldly-wisdom

Saxo Group 'Index funds vs actively managed funds: Which is better for you?'. URL: home.saxo/en-gb/learn/guides/diversification/index-funds-vs-actively-managed-funds-which-is-better-for-you

Chapter 5

Advice on finding a financial adviser:

Citizens Advice: citizensadvice.org.uk/debt-and-money/financial-advice/getting-financial-advice

Financial Conduct Authority: register.fca.org.uk

Money Helper: moneyhelper.org.uk/en

Andy Hart's podcast and blog: mavenadviser.com/podcast; mavenadviser.com/blog

About the author

Andy Hart is a financial adviser and prolific communicator on money and life. As Founder of Maven Adviser, he guides people toward long-term wealth through independent, lifestyle-focused financial planning, evidence-based investing and behavioural-coaching frameworks.

Andy also works with finance professionals through his brand Humans Under Management (HUM). He brings advisers together to sharpen how they serve clients by focusing on behavioural bias, planning discipline and real-world trust. Additionally, he coaches advisers via his platform The Voyantist, helping professionals harness technology, language and mindset to deliver better outcomes.

With a clear mission to take the jargon out of personal finance advice and provide people with the tools to make smart financial decisions, he co-hosts The Real Adviser Podcast (TRAP), as well as having his own show, the Maven Money Personal Finance Podcast.

Outside finance he's a tech enthusiast, world traveller and tennis lover.

Spread the word!

If this book has helped you, there is a good chance it can help someone you care about.

Please recommend it to a friend, share it with a colleague or let others know what you have taken from it. Your support helps these ideas reach the people who need them most.